*The Cock Lane Ghost*

# THE COCK LANE GHOST

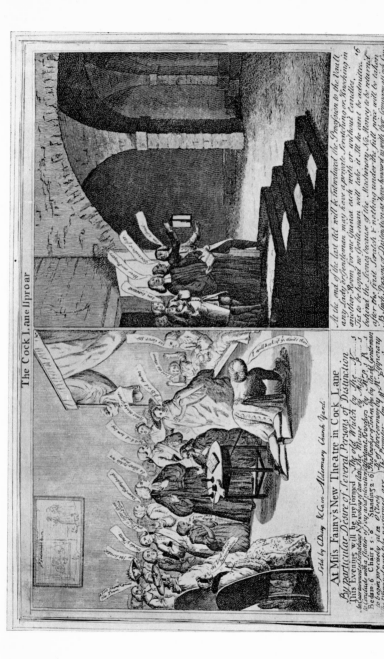

1. 'The Cock Lane Uproar', 1762

# THE
# COCK LANE GHOST

BY

DOUGLAS GRANT

MACMILLAN
London · Melbourne · Toronto

ST MARTIN'S PRESS
New York
1965

MACMILLAN AND COMPANY LIMITED
*Little Essex Street London WC 2*
*also Bombay Calcutta Madras Melbourne*

THE MACMILLAN COMPANY OF CANADA LIMITED
*70 Bond Street Toronto 2*

ST MARTIN'S PRESS INC
*175 Fifth Avenue New York 10010 NY*

PRINTED IN GREAT BRITAIN BY
THE BOWERING PRESS PLYMOUTH

# CONTENTS

# NOTE AND ACKNOWLEDGEMENTS

I HAVE used the following primary sources in this account of the Cock Lane Ghost: the manuscript transcript of the trial of the conspirators (in the Corporation of London Records Office), the Bill brought by John Lynes against William Kent in the Court of Chancery (in the Public Record Office), Frances Lynes's will (in Somerset House), *The Mystery Revealed*, 1762, the pamphlet attributed to Oliver Goldsmith, *Jackson's Oxford Journal, Lloyd's Evening Post, London Chronicle, Public Advertiser, St. James's Chronicle, Annual Register, Beauties of All the Magazines, Gentleman's Magazine, London Magazine, Monthly Chronicle,* and *Universal Magazine.* As my accounts of the seances are usually made up from several of these sources, I have not detailed them in footnotes, for the sake of avoiding interruptions; but the reader is assured that I have taken no liberties with the texts, except to make them conform with each other typographically and occasionally to make them read more easily as dialogue. A further point: the transcript of the trial, among other errors, gives Fanny the surname of 'Lisle', instead of 'Lynes', but this is unquestionably wrong, as her will alone proves.

I have been greatly aided in this essay by Miss Audrey Stead, of Leeds University, who, amongst other help, typed out a difficult 'patchwork' manuscript, and by Miss Anne Baillie, of Macmillan, who procured for me the transcript of the trial.

# LIST OF ILLUSTRATIONS

# I

## EARLY GOTHIC

When the topographer and engraver, J. P. Malcolm, tried to explore the vaults, or crypt, of the parish church of St. John, Clerkenwell, at the end of the eighteenth century, in preparation for his work *Londinium Redivivum*, published in 1803, he got only as far as the entrance before being driven back by the 'horrid sight' and the stench. The sexton was prepared for visitors retreating before the assault of the last, but the phial of lavender-water that he considerately proffered was not enough to make it possible for Malcolm to stand his ground. He consequently missed seeing the vaulting and cross-arches and diagonal ribs, the grooved abaci and chamfered plinths, all twelfth-century work and excellent of their kind; he snatched time only to notice that the coffins were 'immersed in dews' and 'piled and wedged into the shape of the arches'.

The vaults were visited again about fifty years later by another artist, in search of the Gothic decorative detail so much in vogue. They were still in a state of great confusion, but, undeterred, J. W. Archer seated himself on a coffin among the bodies, 'some of which were dried like mummies', and began to sketch a 'picturesque trefoil-headed door' leading into the south vault where he sat working. The sexton's boy held a light up for him to see by.

As he drew, Archer chatted to the boy and was told that the coffin he sat on held the body of 'Scratching Fanny'. He determined at once to investigate, and, with the callousness that often accompanied at that time a superstitious reverence for the dead, he prised open the lid of the coffin to get a glimpse of so notorious a face, the boy tilting the lamp. The face revealed was that of a once-handsome woman. Her nose, Archer noted, was aquiline and still intact: 'an uncommon case, for the cartilage mostly gives way. The remains had become adipocere, and were perfectly preserved.' He studied the features with care, looking for marks of the smallpox from which she was supposed to have died. He could find none. The condition of the face would, however, have been perfectly compatible with death from arsenic poisoning.

Archer was so struck with his discovery that he made particular enquiries before he left from Mr. Bird, the churchwarden, 'a respectable and judicious man'. Bird confirmed that the coffin had always been supposed to hold the body of the 'Cock-Lane woman'.

Long before the time of Archer's investigation, the phrase 'a Cock-lane tale' had become proverbial for a humbug, and how familiar Archer's contemporaries were with the facts of the case, is shown by his temerity in violating a poor woman's coffin. But there are other, less macabre, illustrations of the story being common knowledge. When Thomas Carlyle wished in *Sartor Resartus* to make dramatically the point that we can learn more of the truth of spirits by looking into ourselves than by peering into dark corners for ghosts, he cited Dr. Johnson and the Cock Lane Ghost as such an instance of idle curiosity: 'The English Johnson', he expostulated, 'longed all his life to see a ghost; but could not, though he went to Cock-Lane, and thence to the church-vaults, and tapped on coffins, Foolish Doctor!'

Whether or not the coffin Archer opened was really the one Carlyle imagined Dr. Johnson as tapping on we cannot know. The coffin of the Cock Lane woman never bore a name, and shortly after Archer's visit, in 1860, the vaults were closed for burials and put into decent order, and the coffins were cleared away, hers among the rest.

# II

## THE LODGERS

In October 1759 Richard Parsons, the officiating clerk of St. Sepulchre's, noticed at early prayers a genteel couple standing in the aisle and showed them to a pew. St. Sepulchre's, which stands on the north side of Snow Hill and opposite to where Newgate Prison once stood, is as old a church as St. John's, but even less of the original survives; it was severely damaged in the Great Fire and almost entirely rebuilt in 1670. In 1759 the churchyard, which had been discontinued for burials for about fourteen years, abutted so far into the street on the south side as to make the passage narrow and dangerous. But in this respect it was characteristic of the lanes and over-crowding of West Smithfield.

After the service the couple Parsons had helped thanked him profusely for his civility, and, introducing themselves in the course of conversation as Mr. and Mrs. William Kent, they mentioned they were in search of lodgings. They had been in lodgings near the Mansion House but were leaving after a quarrel with the landlord. Kent had been misguided enough to lend him twenty pounds and had had to arrest him to get its return. Parsons was particularly sympathetic and interested, for he had in fact lodgings of his own for rent in his house in Cock Lane.

4

He took Mr. and Mrs. Kent to view them, and they quickly came to terms.

Richard Parsons is not of the rank to have a recorded history, but he does make one brief appearance, and in rather peculiar circumstances, before he is found talking to Mr. and Mrs. Kent in St. Sepulchre's. An advertisement appeared in the London newspapers on August 5 1756 offering a reward of two guineas from Ann Hind to anyone who could give information leading to the discovery of the writer of an anonymous letter left at Parsons's house. This 'malicious and evil-minded' communication related to the death of Ann Hind's daughter, Sarah, who had just died in Angel Court, Snow Hill, of scarlet fever. Of course, it is impossible to learn now why Mrs. Hind should be so distressed, and how Parsons came to have such a letter delivered to him at his house in Cock Lane.

Cock Lane runs behind St. Sepulchre's to the north, a steep, narrow, winding thoroughfare. Parsons's house may be identified from the drawings made of it in the middle of the nineteenth century, as the one now numbered 20, the offices of J. Lidstone & Son, builders and contractors. It is a plain-fronted house of three stories, with a room to each floor, connected by a winding staircase; too small, one would have thought, for a family to squeeze in lodgers. The house had very much come down in the world by the nineteenth century, when it was serving as the premises of a gas meter maker, and its derelict appearance then might give a wrong impression of the district in the middle of the previous century. The migration of fashion from the City to the West End had long since begun, but much conservative wealth yet remained; John Wilkes, for example, having married the wealthy Miss Mead in 1749, in spite of her age, found himself spending the winter months with his mother-in-law in her house in Red Lion Court, off Cock Lane. The neighbourhood was in decline, but houses like Parsons's were still respectable, and even if room had to be made for lodgers, if they were decent they could rub along in comfort with the family. Parsons had a wife and two daughters; the eldest, Elizabeth, being a child of about ten. Mr. and Mrs. Kent were likely to prove quiet and accommodating lodgers. A baby coming was the obvious assurance of their good behaviour, but there was a further, secret reason. They were not married. And no matter how much they might long to marry, in their anxiety to do so passing themselves off as man and wife, they would never be able to, though neither had the impediment of a living spouse. Not bigamy but the law in another form stood between their union.

Their history was unusual but not exceptional. In 1757 William Kent had married Elizabeth Lynes of Lynham in Norfolk, the daughter of a prosperous grocer. Kent himself later avowed on oath that he and his wife lived in 'great love, harmony, and friendship', and there is good reason to believe him. They may have lived at first at Lynham, but after eleven months they moved elsewhere in Norfolk, to the village of Stoke Ferry, where Kent kept an inn and had taken the post-office. A month after the move Elizabeth died in childbirth.

During Elizabeth's pregnancy her sister Frances — or Fanny, as she was always called — had come to live with her as a companion, and after her death Fanny had stayed on, at first to nurse the baby and, when it shortly followed its mother, to keep house for her desolated brother-in-law. Such a pathetic instance of early bereavement was repeated endlessly up and down the country, at a time when a woman who signed the marriage

2. 'The House and Haunted Room in Cock Lane', by J.W. Archer

(From Charles Mackay's *Memoirs of Extraordinary Popular Delusions*, 1852)

register ran the risk of having her name appear in the mortality bills within the twelve-month.

Kent soon felt himself deeply attracted to Fanny, not least because he thought her very much like his late wife in 'temper and person', and when he found that she had fallen as deeply in love with him as he had with her, he decided to marry her. The only difficulty lay with the law. Fanny Lynes's family may have told him that he could not legally marry his deceased wife's sister. The legal objection temporarily brought to a halt Kent's hope of as good as resuming his interrupted marriage, but on the chance of proving it unsound he made a special journey to London to take the best advice. The counsel to whom he presented his case told him what in fact he must have already known, that Fanny fell within a prohibited degree. Had Elizabeth died without leaving any issue, or had she miscarried and died as a consequence, or had the child been stillborn, Kent would have been permitted to marry Fanny; but the fact that Elizabeth's baby had come into the world alive was an unsurmountable barrier to his happiness. Kent and Fanny had no choice but to part. He decided to give up the post-office and move to London. He left Stoke Ferry in January 1759, intending, as he was a man of some property, to 'purchase a place in some public office', in the hope that 'business would erase that passion he had unfortunately indulged'. Fanny went to live at her brother's in Lynham, and as her family must have known the reason for Kent's departure, and suspected her of weakness and him of designs, her life was probably far from comfortable.

Absence had the customary effect, however, and Fanny began to write him passionate letters from Norfolk, protesting that she was determined to live with him in spite of the consequences, and threatening to follow

him up to London, on foot if necessary. Kent was later to
suggest in self-defence that she was the more eager of the
two to be united. He 'constantly received letters from
the young lady,' he averred, 'filled with repeated entreaties to spend the rest of their lives together'; and 'not-
withstanding this caution of his' in going to London, her
affection 'was not to be stifled or eradicated from her
breast'. As events turned out, he cannot be seriously
blamed for his rather unchivalrous attitude. Nor can
Fanny be blamed for her eagerness; unhappy at home,
and confident of his affection, and trusting in her knowledge of his character, learnt while she was living under
her sister's roof, she could hardly understand why she
should be separated from him by an odd point of
law.

Yielding to her entreaties and his own inclination,
Kent at last decided she should join him. He arranged
that an intimate friend, who was spending a fortnight
in Norfolk at Whitsun 1759, should meet her at Swaffham
and convey her to London. Kent was staying in lodgings
in East Greenwich, and when Fanny joined him there,
they determined that while denied the support and
security of marriage, they would look upon each other
as man and wife. As a proof of their constancy and sin-
cerity they made wills in each other's favour. The advantage in this respect was Fanny's, since she had only 'a
bare hundred pounds' and he had 'a considerable fortune'. Fanny drew up her will on July 7 and after piously
committing her soul into the hands of Almighty God and
her body to the earth, she made bequests of half a crown
apiece to her brothers Thomas and John and her sisters
Catherine, Mary, Susanna and Ann, to be paid within a
month of her decease. She then proceeded to leave
everything she had or might expect, real estate, money,

securities, plate, linen, and clothes, to William Kent, at his 'absolute disposal'. She also appointed him her sole executor; a conspicuous mark of love and trust, which he reciprocated in his own will.

They began at once to live together as man and wife, and as Kent had given himself out to be married before she had ever arrived, they had good reason to suppose that if they acted discreetly and their friends showed equal tact, they might pass undiscovered. But they failed unfortunately to reckon on the enmity of Fanny's family. The family may have disliked Kent as a brother-in-law from the start, but any personal feeling could now have been reinforced by a strong moral disapproval of his action in deliberately choosing to live in sin, in the eyes of both Church and Law; and they could plausibly charge him with taking advantage of the time Fanny had spent in his house to alienate her affections and entice her away. Kent had reason for thinking, however, that if they had had her interests truly at heart, they should have kept quiet. Instead, they let the facts be known, perhaps in order to prevent any suspicion that they had connived in the affair or condoned it. Kent believed that strangers would never have known from his and Fanny's 'mutual happiness and affection' that they were not married, 'had not her relations, who by all the ties of honour and generosity were concerned to keep it a secret, taken every opportunity of divulging it to the world, and, from a pretended regard for her reputation, endeavoured to publish her shame'. Concealment was the more difficult since one of her sisters, Ann, was living in London, in Pall Mall.

Once they had arranged to live together Kent decided to move from Greenwich up to London, where he had a married brother living in the parish of St. Ann's, Alders-

gate.[1] He intended to buy a house, but not finding anything suitable the couple took first the lodgings near the
Mansion House. The best explanation for the landlord
borrowing twenty pounds from Kent is that he needed it
and found him open-handed, but his refusal to repay the
loan, going so far as to hold out until his arrest, is curious.
In view of a report put about later, that he 'did not
approve of Kent's and Fanny's conduct', the suspicion
must be that he learnt of their relation and thought
he could keep the twenty pounds as the price of his
silence. If such was his expectation, he clearly mistook
Kent.

Kent cannot have been gullible, but he had no sooner
moved into Richard Parsons's in Cock Lane than he
agreed to lend Parsons twelve guineas. He may have been
anxious in part to purchase goodwill, but, in view of his
readiness to make loans, he may also have dabbled in
usury while waiting for steadier business to turn up.
Parsons was ready enough to borrow. He was finding it
hard to support his family, but if he was in difficulties he
had only himself to blame. He was known generally as
a very drunken fellow, though otherwise of a respectable
character. In order to make matters easy for him, Kent
agreed that he should repay the loan at the rate of a
guinea a month.

Mr. and Mrs. Kent, as they now called themselves,
were well enough pleased at first with their lodgings.
The terms on which the lodgers lived with their landlord
and his family is shown in the following story. Once,
when Kent was out of London on business — and it
turned out to be a pity that he should ever have had to

[1] According to James Penn, the lecturer of St. Ann's. The sister-in-law
had lived in his household before her marriage. A Thomas Kent and a
Molly Kent were buried in the vaults of St. John's in 1788 and 1792
respectively.

leave her at Parsons's alone — Fanny asked Elizabeth, the older daughter, to sleep with her. Why she should have wanted the child's company when she could have had her servant's, if she was lonely or frightened, is not at all clear. Her servant, Esther Carlisle, nicknamed 'Carrots' on account of her red hair, was an exceptionally honest and reliable girl. But the child and not the servant was preferred as a bedfellow.

Elizabeth slept with her for several nights, and one morning Fanny came down and complained to Mrs. Parsons that they had both been disturbed in the night by the most violent noises. Mrs. Parsons could not for the life of her think what could have been the cause of an occurrence so unusual, but then she remembered their neighbour, an industrious shoemaker. He must have been working late. Nothing happened for a day or two, but on the following Sunday, the one day of the week when quiet might have been expected, the noise broke out again so loudly that Fanny jumped out of bed and called to Mrs. Parsons:

'Pray does your shoemaker work so hard on Sunday nights too?'

'Of course not', was the sense of Mrs. Parsons' reply; whereupon Fanny called to her to come into the room and listen.

An investigation of some kind into these noises is supposed to have been set on foot, and among those invited to come and listen was the Reverend Mr. Linden, but he excused himself. Unfortunately, he died before he could be called on to testify to what he heard said. 'Carrots' was either not there, or having heard nothing was told nothing, a strange lapse in her mistress's confidence. The story of these noises was typical of the many later rumours.

A more verifiable fact was Fanny's condition. She was now six months pregnant, and to assure her of the best attention when her time came, Kent called in Dr. Thomas Cooper, of Northumberland Street, Charing Cross, a doctor of reputation. Cooper first examined her in November, found her health satisfactory, and called to see her at Parsons's once or twice again in the course of the following month. Kent's relations with Parsons, however, had rapidly worsened. Parsons, following the example of his fellow near the Mansion House, refused to repay Kent's loan. Either he drank the guinea a month that he had agreed to repay or he, too, was emboldened by what he had learnt about his lodgers to brave Kent. He made the same mistake as his predecessor. Kent was so unwilling to take any nonsense that he promptly put the matter into the hands of his attorney. He was clearly within his rights, yet his action seems rather precipitate when Parsons can have owed him three guineas at the most, counting until the end of December; and his family affairs might have suggested the wisdom of restraint. He was too ready to make enemies.

Kent was the quicker to proceed to action against Parsons since, in view of the coming baby, he had made arrangements to take a house in Bartlet's Court, off Red Lyon Street, Clerkenwell, not far from St. John's. The rector of St. John's, an acquaintance of Kent's, was the Reverend Stephen Aldrich, a very orthodox priest compared with the Reverend John Moore, the Methodistically inclined lecturer of St. Sepulchre's, where Parsons was clerk. When they came to leave Parsons's in January the house in Bartlet's Court was not ready, and Kent and Fanny had to move temporarily into an inconvenient apartment near by, belonging to Mr. Hunt, a jeweller. As they were hardly stopping, however, a little discomfort was easily borne, even for a woman now eight months gone.

Fanny woke on January 25 thinking her time had come and, interpreting an acute pain in her back as the beginnings of labour, she sent for Dr. Cooper. Cooper quickly discovered that she was not in labour, but neither Fanny herself nor 'the women about her' believed him. He judged from her symptoms that she was suffering the early stages of an eruptive fever, and knowing that if such were the case she would be ill for some time, at a most critical turn of her life, he agreed to Kent's suggestion that she should be carried to the house in Bartlet's Court, especially since Hunt's lodgings were so unsuitable for an invalid. Dr. Cooper himself superintended her removal by coach in the afternoon, making quite sure she was protected against cold. 'I had her immediately put to bed,' he later testified; 'ordered her to be blooded, and prescribed such cordial medicines as I thought were proper to throw out an eruption; a nurse was immediately provided, and all necessaries for the care of the sick patient.' As Fanny looked about her as they carried her into her new home from the coach and up to bed, and saw the thorough preparations being taken for her recovery, she must have thought how right she had been to trust Kent as a husband. Kent, in his turn, cannot have helped but look back anxiously to the similar scenes of less than two years ago, in which the chief part had been played by Fanny's sister, Elizabeth.

The following day Dr. Cooper called on her again, and met there, by appointment, her apothecary, James Jones, of Grafton Street, Soho. The severe lumbago in the back and the other symptoms now pointed in only one direction, and Dr. Cooper was forced to diagnose what he appears reluctant to have recognized the day before, smallpox; a confluent smallpox 'of a very virulent nature'. Kent was immediately told of the seriousness of her condition. She was blistered and dosed with cordial medicines and treated with every attention; and for four or five days she seemed to be holding her own, but 'when maturation should have been performed' — in Dr. Cooper's medical jargon — 'the pulse flagged, the fever sank, and the whole eruption put on a wharty, pallid appearance.'

Fanny herself was now fully aware of her danger, and her first thought was to make sure that the will she had made in Kent's favour upon coming to London was good. She sent for Mr. Morse, an attorney, and was assured by him that everything she possessed was effectually secured to Kent, as she had intended. By this insistence she proved her love of and gratitude to Kent, but, like him in the matter of the loans to his landlords, she might have been better advised to have been less businesslike, especially at the expense of her family. She was now finding it increasingly difficult to swallow, and as she began visibly to decline, Kent was advised that she could hardly live more than a few days.

The news of Fanny's illness was known about the neighbourhood. The row with Parsons over the loan entitled Parsons to tell all that he knew about Kent's and Fanny's relationship; and if he himself did not make the deduction, there were others ready to interpret her illness as a visitation of God upon sinners and to follow its course with superstitious interest. And there was other and more sinister evidence to suggest that all was not well.

James Franzen, the publican of the 'Wheat Sheaf' in Cock Lane, knew that Parsons's house was haunted; at least, he had been told by both Parsons and his wife of the mysterious noises which were first heard on the nights when Fanny lay with Elizabeth Parsons, and which Mrs. Parsons had then attributed to a shoemaker. They had since been resumed, after Kent and Fanny had left the lodgings. One night when Fanny was lying seriously ill in Bartlet's Court, Franzen called on Parsons and, finding him out, sat with Mrs. Parsons and her daughter. The strange noises began here and there about the room, and sounded to Franzen 'like knuckles knocking against the wainscot'. He was assured that they now came every night.

Franzen was extremely frightened and being convinced that the house was indeed haunted he got up to go home. But as he opened the kitchen door 'he saw pass by him something in white, seemingly in a sheet, which shot by him and upstairs.' The light emitted by the figure was sufficiently bright to throw a beam through a window and illuminate momentarily the face of the clock in the charity school across the way. In spite of his fear, Franzen would have followed the shape, but Elizabeth shut the door and warned him he had better not. Deeply shaken, Franzen took his leave and went home. As he sat by his kitchen fire trying to recover his nerve, and still too afraid to go to bed, there was a sudden knocking on the door. He was at first too frightened to stir, but on forcing himself to open the door he found Parsons himself outside, in a terrible state of fright:

'Give me the largest glass of brandy you have!' Parsons exclaimed breathlessly as he rushed in.

'Why what's the matter?'

'Oh, Franzen! as I was going into my house just now I saw the Ghost!'

'And so did I!' groaned Franzen; 'and have been greatly frightened ever since. Bless me! What can be the meaning of it? it is very unaccountable.'

They were both so agitated that they needed more brandy before parting.

The matter was not as unaccountable as Franzen supposed. Parsons was able to enlighten him. As Fanny Lynes was still a-dying the ghost could consequently not be hers; it must be the ghost of her lamented sister Elizabeth. Elizabeth's restless spirit was the cause of the noises that were an increasing disturbance in Parsons's house.

Poor Fanny — her condition was now hopeless, and Dr. Cooper advised Kent to send for a minister of religion. The Reverend Stephen Aldrich of St. John's waited on her and out of his goodness and charity tried to reassure her that there would be forgiveness even for her sin — a sin that was to cease to be within a hundred years. He did what he could, too, to comfort Kent. Fanny began to weaken rapidly; for fifty hours before she died she hardly took more than a pint of liquid, and then only under the administration of the doctor or the apothecary, and on the last day her speech failed and her mind began to wander. She died on the evening of February 2, 1760.

Kent was now faced with the melancholy duty of burying a second wife, for such he had sincerely considered Fanny to be; and Stephen Aldrich could witness that during his several visits he had never seen 'a grief more expressive or a tenderness more affecting'. In accordance with the terms of Fanny's will, which had specifically enjoined him as sole executor to give her body decent interment, Kent ordered the undertaker 'to make as good a coffin as he could, both lined and covered'. He asked for no name to be put on the coffin, fearing that if he gave Fanny his own he might be prosecuted, but when he came to register the burial, and found that he must give a name, he gave her his own, 'being determined she should not suffer reproach, whatever might be the result'.

He notified her family and particularly her sister Ann, who was living in Pall Mall. Ann came, and though it was later to be stated by Kent's enemies that the coffin was already screwed down before she arrived, Kent was able to rely on witnesses and assert that Ann spent some time weeping over Fanny's body while it lay still exposed. Kent offered her a part or all of Fanny's clothes, but she refused, saying that Kent was entitled to all of Fanny's possessions. The funeral ceremonies decently but discreetly concluded, the body of Frances Lynes was laid to rest in the vaults of St. John's, Clerkenwell.

When Ann Lynes learnt the terms of Fanny's will, which left her and her brothers and sisters half a crown apiece and all the rest to Kent, she tried by entering a caveat to prevent Kent from proving the will in Doctors' Commons, on February 6, four days after Fanny's death. The will was legally invulnerable, but to the Lynes family Kent had clearly influenced Fanny to draw it up exclusively in his favour and had acted 'in prejudice of her brother and sisters, who lived in great harmony and love together, before this fatal accident'.

# III

# KNOCK ONE, KNOCK TWO

With Fanny dead and buried, William Kent put the unhappy past behind him and set about rebuilding his shattered domestic life, and resuming a career. He set up as a stockbroker and it may have been through business that he met the woman whom he married in about the middle of 1761. At the end of the year, he was negotiating to go into partnership with her brother. She was supposed to have a fortune of about £3,000. She and her family may very probably have been told nothing in detail of Fanny Lynes; if Kent described himself as a widower he was telling no more than the strict truth. He could not have been expected to handicap himself with her memory; let the dead bury their dead.

Fanny's memory, however, was to be brought uncomfortably alive by an unforeseen consequence of her will. In her anxiety to endow Kent with all she had, she had specifically mentioned her expectations on the death of her elder brother Thomas. Thomas was alive when she drew up her will, but he may have been ill at the time, and he certainly died within six weeks, on August 19, 1759. Fanny and each of her sisters received £150 each, and Fanny's share constituted the bulk of the money Kent inherited under her will. But Thomas had also left some land to be sold and the profits divided among his beneficiaries, and on November 8, 1760, £378 10s. 4d. was shared out, an equal proportion, £94 12s. 7d., falling to William Kent as Fanny's executor. The family obviously resented Kent's claim.

The ill-feelings stirred up might still have been allowed to lapse had it not been for an unfortunate mistake. The land that John Lynes had sold, as executor to his brother Thomas, he had sold as freehold, when it was in fact only copyhold. The purchaser naturally demanded compensation, and at a meeting of Thomas Lynes's beneficiaries held at the 'Unicorn' in Mileham, Norfolk, on May 20, 1761, it was agreed to pay £45 in compensation and to require the beneficiaries to refund John Lynes this sum in equal proportions. Kent did not attend the meeting, and when he was asked for his share of the £45 he refused to pay, alleging that he had already spent the money in settling Fanny Lynes's debts.

Whatever grounds he may have had in self-interest or personal irritation, or even justice — though on the face of it he had hardly a case — for taking this step, he was most ill-advised not to have agreed to act as the other beneficiaries had done. John Lynes had recourse to law and on October 31, 1761, he began proceedings in Chancery to make Kent repay his proportion.

Matters were no more quiet elsewhere, but it would have been extremely hard to discover what exactly was happening. Some time in 1760 Richard Parsons's eldest daughter, Elizabeth, had convulsive fits, and was attended by Mr. Gammon, an apothecary. And the noises in Parsons's house were intermittently continued. People in the neighbourhood all knew about them and several had heard them. When Joyce Wetheral, one of the neighbours, came to hear them and asked Parsons the cause, he said — disingenuously, in view of his earlier explanation to Franzen — that he believed it must be thieves. But the noises were more than a mystification or a scarey diversion, they were becoming a nuisance. Catherine Friend, a lodger at Parsons's after Kent and Fanny had left, not being able to place the noises, spoke to Parsons, but Parsons complained of them himself. Miss Friend left when she found they could not be stopped.

Parsons went to some lengths to prove that he had no hand in the mystery. He called in a carpenter, Bateman Griffiths, and told him to take down the wainscoting. Nothing was found and Griffiths nailed the wainscot back. Such a drastic investigation demonstrated that Parsons was deeply puzzled himself and seriously determined to get to the bottom of the matter; and it also showed that the noises could not originate in any natural source. They must be the work of another kind of agency.

As the officiating clerk of St. Sepulchre's, it would have been most unusual for Richard Parsons not to have taken a problem that trenched upon the spiritual to one of the clergy. He decided to approach John Moore, the lecturer — the assistant preacher, an elective office — of St. Sepulchre's since 1754, and, since June 1761, the rector of St. Bartholomew the Great, in West Smithfield. Moore was in every respect a man of good character, deeply respected in many quarters; the only thing that could be held against him was that though he was devout, his devotion was Methodistical. Parsons discussed the noises with him and having aroused his interest he sent for him one night at ten o'clock when they were particularly obstreperous. Moore hurried round and from that time forward became deeply involved in their interpretation.

What was the cause of the knockings? This was the

question it was absolutely necessary to determine. As all the possibilities of an ordinary agent had been explored, it could only be a spirit; and such a conjecture was strongly supported by the recollection of the ghost that had been seen when Fanny Lynes lay on her deathbed, and was supposed to have been the ghost of her sister, Elizabeth. The spirit now troubling Parsons's house, by the force of association, must be that of Fanny herself; and if the spirits of two women were restlessly coming back to earth in turn and persistently calling attention to themselves, it must be because they had information to give and would not rest quiet until they had been understood.

The idea that a spirit might revisit 'the glimpses of the moon' to impart a solemn message was as commonly held in the eighteenth century as it had been in the previous century, at the time of the first production of *Hamlet*; in spite of materialism and scepticism it was widespread among the educated classes. One of the commonest charges levelled against the early Methodists was that in their battle with infidelity they deliberately played upon credulity and encouraged superstition in order to prove that the spiritual lay immediately to hand. They interpreted the hysteria and hallucinations that accompanied their missions as visible evidence of grace abounding and divine possession; they discovered in every unusual happening, from a cloudburst to a broken leg, signs of intervening Providence; and demons and witches and apparitions were anxiously expected as witnesses to the truth of another world. Their enemies accused them of hypocrisy, but however many hypocrites lurked among them, the majority were simply gullible and credulous, including John Wesley himself. 'He accredited and repeated stories of apparitions, and witchcraft, and possession', Robert Southey remarked — commenting upon what he called 'his voracious credulity'—'so silly, as well as monstrous, that they might have nauseated the coarsest appetite for wonder'. Wesley's defence of his readiness to believe would have been similar to the excuse offered by his sister, Emily, when she had to explain her attitude to an instance of the preternatural: 'I am so far from being superstitious', she wrote, 'that I was too much inclined to infidelity, so that I heartily rejoice at having such an opportunity of convincing myself, past doubt or scruple, of the existence of some things besides those we see.'

The occurrence to which Emily Wesley was referring was, oddly enough, a knocking spirit, 'Old Jeffrey', as she came to nickname him. Towards the end of 1715 a maid-servant, new to the household of the Reverend Samuel Wesley of Epworth, heard mysterious groans from the dining-room. The groans were followed by knockings and similar disturbances in other parts of the house. Sometimes the noises were like bottles being clashed together, or a man trampling up and down stairs, or the gobbling of a turkey cock, but usually they sounded like knockings, three or four blows at a time. Mrs. Wesley thought they might be caused by rats and having heard of rats being driven out by the sounding of a horn, she had a horn blown loudly in each room in turn for half a day. The uproar so antagonized 'Old Jeffrey' that he began to knock in the daytime too, sometimes with extreme violence. The goblin, or poltergeist, was easily angered: by the hunting-horn, of course, but also by Samuel Wesley rebuking him as 'a deaf and dumb devil' for troubling innocent children, and telling him to come to his study, if he had anything to say. 'Old Jeffrey' took him at his word, and Wesley was the only person actually

3. Cock Lane, 1964

pushed by him. He would sometimes answer knock for
knock, but more than a simple pattern puzzled him. He
was seen twice; once in shape like a badger and again
like a white rabbit, with its ears back and its scut up
straight. John Wesley was away at school when these
happenings took place, but he was later to draw up and
publish an account of them. He credited them, of course,
implicitly, and would have echoed his father's comment
at the time, that though Providence's design in permit-
ting 'Old Jeffrey' might not be understood, 'secret things
belong to God', and wisdom and duty were 'to prepare
seriously for all events'. S. T. Coleridge looked elsewhere
than to Providence for an explanation; he attributed
such phenomena to 'a contagious nervous disease, the
acme or intensest form of which is catalepsy'.

The spirit that had begun to knock so purposefully in
Cock Lane could not have had a finer ancestor, Methodistically speaking, than 'Old Jeffrey', and its visitation
coincided with a period of intense and successful mis-
sionary activity by the Methodists, both in and out of
London. 'This year, from beginning to end,' John
Wesley exclaimed, 'was a year never to be forgotten.
Such a season I never saw before.' They were bound to
be suspected by those who detested their activities, of
joining to put up the Ghost, especially as some of their
prominent members were involved.

As soon as the Reverend John Moore had been brought
in by Richard Parsons and had taken on the Ghost's
management, they set about discovering its intentions
by devising a system of question and answer. The obvious
way to get a dumb spirit to answer questions was to
propose, as Samuel Wesley had to 'Old Jeffery', that
it should signify itself by knocks. Moore and Parsons between them came to an agreement with the Ghost that

a single knock should signify the affirmative, a double knock the negative. The Ghost concluded independently that it would express displeasure by scratching. They had no difficulty in making the Ghost stand for questions. The noises may have sounded in the beginning haphazardly around the house, but they had now become associated exclusively with Elizabeth, the older Parsons girl. Wherever she went the Ghost went too, and made its presence known, especially at night, after Elizabeth and her sister had been put to bed.

The preliminary questioning established that the Ghost had returned to earth to repeat the old and terrible tale of ghosts — of offended innocence and 'murder most foul, strange, and unnatural', walking abroad unpunished. The spirit which had appeared in white and terrified James Franzen had always been assumed to be the ghost of Elizabeth Kent, and now it was conjectured that it had appeared when it did in order to give warning that Fanny Lynes was about to suffer the same fate as Elizabeth. Had she not been murdered by her husband, William Kent? The charge that Kent had murdered his first wife was never pressed, the ghostly witness having withdrawn itself, and this first and shadowy crime was forgotten as the neighbours who were beginning to frequent the seances in Cock Lane learnt circumstantially of Kent's other atrocious offence from the ghost of Fanny Lynes, for she it was who knocked. By trial and error, by question and answer, patiently and designedly put, the Ghost's knockings were proved conclusively to relate how Fanny had died by poison, administered to her in purl — an infusion of bitter herbs in beer or ale; a popular restorative — by William Kent about two hours before she died. She had returned to earth to knock for justice to be done.

The Reverend John Moore had learnt much about Kent from Richard Parsons, and how vindictively he had pursued him over a trivial sum, and now Fanny's relations, with fresh evidence of Kent's obduracy at hand, came forward to tell him more. Having either learnt or, more likely, been told about the Ghost, Ann Lynes, the sister in Pall Mall, affirmed that she had been 'deprived of the pleasure of seeing her dear sister's body, as the coffin had been screwed down some time before she came to the house', thereby strengthening the suspicion of foul play — smallpox would have been evident enough! Moore was religiously disposed to take the Ghost on trust, but in view of the seriousness of the charge it was levelling, he felt he needed the support of his fellow clergymen, and among the several that he called in was the Reverend Thomas Broughton. Broughton was lecturer at both St. Helen's, Bishopsgate Within, and All Hallows, Lombard Street, secretary to the Society for Promoting Christian Knowledge, and an early Methodist. He visited the Ghost on January 5 and was quite unable to locate where the knocks came from in answer to his questions. He left convinced of the Ghost's authenticity. The charges harboured against Kent by the Ghost were now bound to be more widely known.

Kent himself was faced with the troublesome bill in Chancery but remained quite unaware of the happenings at Parsons's house, until in the early days of January the same friend who had accompanied Fanny Lynes up to London called on him with a copy of the *Public Ledger*.[1] In the paper was an advertisement that purported to tell of 'the bringing of a young lady out of Norfolk to a

[1] Unfortunately, complete files of the *Public Ledger* are not available, and none contains any numbers for 1762. I have had consequently to collect the matter that first appeared in its pages from other sources, usually other newspapers.

prison at Greenwich, &c., and that it was supposed she was murdered by poison which was given her in some purl'. The effect of this paragraph upon Kent was electric.

> Mr. Kent said upon seeing and reading this paragraph he was very much confused and frightened, could not conceive what could be the meaning of it, and was so affected at the thoughts of such an advertisement that he retired to his chamber to give vent to the passions and commotions in his breast arising from such an accusation, when he was convinced he had behaved in the most kind and affectionate manner to her till her death; however he with the help and advice of his friends recovered his spirits.

Kent was not to keep his recovered spirits for long. A day or two later he read in the same newspaper, the *Public Ledger*, another advertisement giving an account of the Ghost in Cock Lane and of the questions that were being put to it. If he was frightened before, he was terrified now; he was being publicly arraigned by a ghost of murder.

Kent learnt from the advertisement that the Reverend John Moore 'was the person to apply to', and went immediately to call on him, taking a witness. After expressing his surprise that a clergyman should get involved in such an affair, and bluntly warning him that if he went on in it 'he would suffer for it in the end', Kent asked to see the questions actually put to the Ghost, which on Moore's admission had been drawn up between him and Parsons. Moore at first refused to show him the list until they were alone, but at last he gave in and read it to him. When he came to the question asking the Ghost whether or not she had been married to Kent, Moore stopped and enquired whether in fact he and Fanny had been married. Kent acknowledged they had not and gave the reason, that his wife had been survived by a child. A little disconcerted by Kent's frankness, Moore hesitated and began to admit that he himself did not think Kent had murdered Fanny, but these visitations must at least be considered as a judgment on him. Moore assured him that 'there were very strange noises of knockings and scratchings every night, and that there was something behind darker than all the rest, and that if he would go to Parsons's house, he might be a witness to the same and convinced of its reality'.

Kent's only sensible course was to attend a seance as Moore had suggested, and the same evening of January 12 he went to Cock Lane, taking with him Dr. Cooper and Mr. Jones, the doctor and the apothecary, who had attended Fanny during her fatal illness. The Reverend Thomas Broughton also went with them. The formalities of the seance had by this time been settled. At Elizabeth Parsons's bedtime, she was publicly undressed and put to bed with her younger sister 'with proper solemnity'. The bedroom was a very small one, on the upper floor, but the bed was stood in the middle to allow the audience to sit all round and admit as many as possible. As the Ghost had been discovered to be sensitive to incredulity and ridicule, those attending were warned that unless they showed a proper respect she would be angry and refuse to manifest herself by knocking at all. The part of interrogator was usually taken by Mary Frazer, an elderly servant with not the best of reputations.

As soon as the child was made ready, and the audience were settled, with Kent and his friends placed prominently among them, Mary Fraser came in and began running about the room, crying:

'Fanny, Fanny, why don't you come? Do come, pray Fanny, come; dear Fanny, come!'

Nothing happened, in spite of Mary's blandishments. Moore then told them the Ghost refused to come because they were making too much noise. 'She was a sulky touchy thing,' he explained, 'and they must take her as she run.' But if they would go and wait downstairs, he would see if he could raise her by stamping at her with his foot. They dutifully trooped downstairs, and after about ten minutes of stamping Moore returned to tell them that she had come and to ask them to go up again. As he had promised, the Ghost had begun to knock, and Kent, with a feeling of suppressed horror and trepidation, asked him to put the questions to it that he had read over earlier in the day. Moore agreed, but first he told Kent: 'You must observe one knock is an affirmative and two a negative, for so Parsons and I have settled it.' The questioning was then begun.

> 'Are you the wife of Mr. Kent?' — Two knocks.
> 'Did you die naturally?' — Two knocks.
> 'By poison?' — One knock.
> 'Did any person other than Mr. Kent administer it?' — Two knocks.
> 'Was it given in water-gruel, beer, or any other liquor?' — Knocked for beer, which was later changed to purl.
> 'How long did you live after receiving it?' — Three knocks, one for each hour.
> 'Did Carrots know of you being poisoned?' — One knock.
> 'Should Mr. Kent be taken up?' — One knock.

Without being given a chance to reply, Kent now heard himself openly charged for the first time, by an invisible accuser, with the murder of Fanny Lynes, and his consternation became the greater when one of the others in the room said, 'Kent, ask this Ghost if you shall be hanged'. He put the question and was answered with a single knock.

'Thou art a lying spirit,' he expostulated at this final provocation; 'thou are not the ghost of my Fanny. She would never have said any such thing.'

But no outburst on Kent's part, however sincere, could repel the Ghost's deadly charges, and action would have to be taken quickly if Kent was going to protect his reputation, without taking into account the more unlikely danger of the threat to his life.

The Ghost was rapidly becoming notorious and drew increasingly large crowds from the neighbourhood to the seances, and her popularity increased when it was found that she would accompany Elizabeth Parsons wherever she was moved. On Thursday, January 14, two days after Kent's interview, Elizabeth was taken to the house of a Mr. Bray in the neighbourhood and put to bed with a servant, but in spite of this precaution the knockings continued. They sounded, according to Miss Bray, to be coming from behind the wainscot and from other parts of the room, but not from the bed at all where the child lay.

Mr. Bray took the opportunity of asking the Ghost several questions, the following among them:

'Are you a good spirit?' he enquired. — One knock.
'Do you come from God?' — One knock.

The questions were in character. Bray was later to testify that 'Whilst she was at my house two noblemen knowing she was with me and that (thank God) I was a man of good character, they came to my house to hear the noises and did several times.' Bray, unfortunately, did not choose to identify his noble guests, but one of them was almost certainly William Legge, Earl of Dartmouth, a Methodist sympathizer. Horace Walpole once saw him at a service at the Magdalen House, the charity for reformed prostitutes, sitting with his wife 'in the odour of devotion'. He had decided to make an enquiry into the Ghost a particular interest. Both Bray and his daughter believed that under the circumstances in which they heard them, the noises must be preternatural.

The affair had so far only been mentioned publicly in the *Public Ledger*, the medium chosen by the Ghost's supporters to justify her and make her known, but once the houses where she was to be heard had become the haunt of noblemen, the other papers quickly followed suit, and after a moment of copying from the *Ledger*'s columns began to publish their own independent and increasingly full reports. Both the *London Chronicle* and the *St. James's Chronicle* first referred to the Ghost in their numbers for January 16 to 19, and *Lloyd's Evening Post* in its number for January 18 to 20. This was the critical weekend; from then on the Ghost was committed to performing before a swelling audience, and no withdrawal of the charges being urged against Kent was possible. Crowds from all quarters of the town flocked to Cock Lane, stopping the narrow way with coaches and pestering anyone who had first-hand information to give. The group of credulous clergymen and pious dilettanti could hardly find peace to continue their interrogations.

After lying a few days at Mr. Bray's and learning to keep good company, the girl was returned to her father's, and on Monday, January 18, Kent again attended a seance, taking with him this time Stephen Aldrich of St. John's and Mr. Jones, the apothecary, as well as several others. The interview was very fully reported in the papers.

When they were shown upstairs they were warned to be quiet for fear of disturbing the spirit, who had already begun to scratch. Mary Frazer acted as the interpreter.

'Are you come, my dear? Pray tell me what it is o'clock? — A scratch followed, which implied displeasure.

'Do, my dear, don't be ill-natured, tell me what it is o'clock? — Ten knocks were given.

'And how much after?' — One knock was given for a quarter. ['Here the spirit was mistaken, it being thirty-five minutes after,' is the reporter's precise comment.]

'A gentleman present got up, stamped with his foot by the bedside; on which she (the spirit) scratched; which they continued for some time, stamping and scratching. At last the gentleman sat down.'

She was then asked if she would answer more questions, and having concurred with a knock, the interview was continued.

'Is Mr. Kent in the room?' — One knock.

'Have you been seen by anybody?' — One knock.

'Have you been seen by Mr. Parsons and his daughter and Mr. Franzen?' — One knock.

'As you have been seen by them, will you not show yourself to the persons present?' — Two knocks.

'If Mr. Kent was left in the room alone, would you not appear to him?' — Two knocks.

The questions that were really to the purpose were again put to her: had she been married to Kent? had he murdered her? had he poisoned her? should he be arrested? The replies were in each instance again emphatic and malevolent.

At this point a clergyman took up a candle to look under the bed, but the Ghost refused to answer the next question. Mary Frazer explained that she had now disappeared, 'she loving not light'. She returned in about five minutes however and having signified her presence by scratching, the questioning started again.

'How many clergymen are there present?' — One knock. ['Here the spirit was again mistaken, for there were two; but this was cleared up by a gentleman's observing, that the second clergyman was a stranger to her.']

'How many persons were present?' — Six knocks: right.

'Will you answer Mr. Kent?' — Scratched hard, angrily; but being again intreated, gave one knock.

'Was she Fanny?' Kent asked. — One knock.

'Can I be of any service to you?' Aldrich asked. — Two knocks. She clearly had discrimination enough to recognize her friends and foes.

'Can I?' Moore asked. — One knock.

'Can I be of service in getting Mr. Kent convicted?' Moore persisted, with simplicity bordering on malice. — One knock. Aldrich merrily tried to put a further question:

'Would she appear in a court of judicature?' Mary Frazer refused to relay it.

'If you are really a spirit,' a layman present asked, 'knock on this bedpost,' rapping on the post with a stick. The result was angry scratches.

The questions that followed became increasingly frivolous as the audience tried in vain to catch the Ghost out, or to make it prove its authenticity in ways within the compass of its limited range of expression and manœuvre. People were bound to become bewildered and dissatisfied.

The additional fact that appeared to have been learnt from this interview was that the Ghost counted upon Fanny Lynes's servant, Esther Carlisle ('Carrots') to support her assertion that Fanny had been poisoned. Moore and Parsons were as much in a dilemma as Kent. If he was yet unable to clear himself from suspicion, they were unable to bring their charges home. They required independent evidence to corroborate the word of the Ghost. Under the circumstances of Fanny's death, 'Carrots' alone was likely to tell them what they wanted to know. 'Carrots' had moved to a new position after Fanny's death, but James Franzen found her out and brought her to Moore on January 19.

'Carrots' had heard nothing of the mysterious happenings, and Moore had first to explain to her that the house was haunted, supposedly by the ghost of her late mistress.

'You are the only one that can be evidence to Kent's poisoning your mistress by putting poison in some purl,' Moore went on, 'for your mistress's ghost says she told you so a short time before she died.'

'Bless me, sir,' Carrots exclaimed in amazement, 'my mistress could not speak before she died for four days.'

'Ah,' said Moore acutely, 'she said so, though perhaps you might not understand her; and to convince you, you shall hear her say so yourself.'

Moore then arranged with her that she should attend the seance in the evening. She arrived early and as soon as Moore came in with Mrs. Parsons, Mary Frazer and some others, he said to her:

'Carrots, these noises have been heard and this house has been troubled with these noises this three years, and it is thought to be the spirit of your mistress; and she says that she took poison two or three hours before she died, and that you are able to give some information of her being poisoned because she told you of it a short time before she died.'

'She never told me any such thing I'm sure,' Carrots exclaimed; 'my master and mistress were very loving, and lived very happy together.'

'Why!' Moore said, finding her less compliant than he had hoped and trying a more ordinary tack, 'the Ghost says, if you was taken up and carried before a magistrate you could give some account of the murder, for she told nobody but you.'

'I know nothing of it,' Carrots replied.

When Moore insisted that she must know and asked her to tell the truth, she sturdily repeated that she did not understand what he meant by the truth; she knew nothing of the matter. Then she added, with the honest craft of those who must battle to survive, that she had a new place to go to and must go then and there.

'Nay,' Moore exclaimed, finding threats were useless, 'stay now; come tell the truth and you shall be provided for; don't fear for a place.'

'Carrots' may have smelt the bribe, but she had clearly forfeited her excuse.

At about ten o'clock Kent arrived, anxious to learn what new twist was now to be given to his fortunes; with him were James Franzen, the Reverend William Dodd, the dandified chaplain to the Magdalen House, a popular preacher, unlikely to miss such an opportunity of figuring before the public,[1] and Thomas Broughton. Altogether there were about twenty people in the room, including two negroes; and of course an uncounted number of spectators in the passageways and in the lane below. The bed was first thoroughly examined, and the bedclothes, and when the auditors were satisfied there was no visible evidence of a cheat, the two children were undressed and tucked in. The bed itself was found to be unsteady, but this was not considered material.

When matters were conveniently settled Mary Frazer began her usual coaxing of the Ghost.

'Fanny, Fanny,' she called, knocking on the wainscot, 'are you coming, Fanny? Are you coming, my dear lady?' Thus she went on, running about the room and knocking. 'If you don't come, I will go directly.'

Moore was somehow irritated by this performance to-night and told her to leave the room. As she went a scratching was heard. 'She was a touchy lady and sulky and she must be took as she run', Moore said, repeating his phrases by rote, but he would try to bring her if the others would wait downstairs. In a short time the knock-

[1] Franzen referred in his evidence to a Mr. Dodd being present, and judging by the number of clergy given as present in the newspapers, 'Mr. Dodd' was very probably the Reverend William Dodd, later hanged for forgery.

ing was heard and Moore called them up. Upon the Ghost being asked if she would answer questions and her replying in the affirmative, the seance with 'Carrots' as principal and Moore as interrogator began.

'Is Carrots in the room?' Moore asked. — One knock.

'Does Carrots know any thing of the murder?' — One knock.

'Is your murderer here?' — One knock.

'If Carrots and her master were taken up and carried before a magistrate would they confess?' — One knock.

At this point, when the tension in the room had mounted unbearably as the charge against Kent was so emphatically reaffirmed, and a mysterious sound like a fluttering of wings, the sign of the Ghost's being pleased, had already been heard in the room, 'Carrots' asked if she might question the Ghost herself.

'Are you my mistress?' she demanded directly. — One knock.

But the knock was immediately followed by the noise of scratching, which showed that the Ghost was deeply angered at having her identity questioned.

'Are you angry with me, Madam?' 'Carrots' asked incredulously. — One knock.

'Then I am sure, Madam,' 'Carrots' replied, 'you may be ashamed of yourself for I never hurt you in my life.'[1]

'Carrots's' sharp and honest retort brought the judicial sitting of the evening to an end, and the company went below, leaving only James Franzen and Mary Frazer alone in the room. Franzen was, on his own admission, so 'vastly frightened' that he could hardly move.

[1] The reporter who took down the evidence in court made a marginal note at this point: 'Carrots appeared to be a simple honest girl, for when she was talking to the supposed Ghost, she talked as if her mistress had been incarnate, saying, Yes Madam and Madam each time of speaking.'

'Do you think the Ghost will come again?' he asked his companion timidly.

'Oh, it will come soon,' Mary Frazer replied; 'let us go to prayers.'

Franzen was rather astonished at this, knowing her 'to be a bad woman', but Mary Frazer, having learnt from the Methodists how to play the saint, picked up a Book of Common Prayer and began repeating the Lord's Prayer.

'Why don't you pray?' she asked Franzen.

Poor Franzen could only protest that he wished he could, but he was too frightened.

'Damnation! I'll fetch her presently,' Frazer rapped out, Prayer Book in hand.

Sure enough, the noise was heard again and Franzen 'was so much afraid that he asked the Ghost, whether or no he should be frightened to death?' One knock was given.[1]

The open seance continued throughout the night until four o'clock in the morning, when the Ghost, having found in Franzen a victim fit to hand, followed him back the few yards to the 'Wheat Sheaf' and terrified him and his wife by knocking in their bedchamber.

[1] The court reporter wryly noted as he took down Franzen's evidence: 'Poor Franzen hardly seemed recovered from his fright in court.'

# IV

## A LORD MAYOR'S LOT

THE Ghost had now done everything that lay immediately within her power. She had brought her charges against Kent with unequalled force of publicity; and in the eyes of John Moore and Thomas Broughton and the Methodists, having dramatically asserted the spiritual world, she must now surely touch the hardened consciences of Kent and his accomplice 'Carrots', and drive them at last into open confession. The idea of such a triumphant vindication of their faith was more than enough to make them press on with their questioning of obliging Fanny; surely she would, in the manner of Providence, when their hopes were at their lowest, suddenly work in Kent that long-deferred change of heart, or, if he remained obdurate, produce evidence to put the crime beyond doubt.

Kent himself, having the impossible task of coming to grips with an invisible and insubstantial adversary, could only defeat her charge by proving that the manifestations were a malicious imposture, set on foot by a conspiracy. His open enemies, Richard Parsons and the Lynes family, had not yet witnessed his destruction, but they had at least the satisfaction of knowing that the Ghost had caused him illimitable distress at home, by suggesting to his new wife and her family that he was a man of the worst possible character, and abroad, by damaging his reputation in a way to ruin him in business. He had been negotiating earlier with his new brother-in-law to go into partnership with him, but such plans had now to be postponed indefinitely. He was the centre of what had become a major public scandal, with the crowds flocking to Cock Lane in such numbers, by day as well as night, that Parsons had to shut up his house. The pious and the dissipated competed. 'The Methodists have promised them [the promoters of the Ghost] contributions'; Horace Walpole wrote ironically to George Montagu: 'provisions are sent in like forage, and all the taverns and ale-houses in the neighbourhood make fortunes.' James Franzen found that the 'Wheat Sheaf' paid as never before, the credulous swallowing down with his beer his tales of terror.

On Wednesday, January 20, the night following 'Carrots's' confrontation with the Ghost, a further seance was held in the house of Mr. Bruin, a pawnbroker, which stood at the corner of Hosier Lane, in the neighbourhood. Bruin had been convinced of the Ghost's veracity by its answering correctly, with one knock, his question, How many pieces of money had he given to a poor acquaintance?

Among those who attended on this occasion was a gentleman 'extremely desirous of detecting the fraud, and discovering the truth of this mysterious affair', who contributed an account to the *London Chronicle*. He arrived with his party, which included the Reverend James Penn, the lecturer of St. Ann's, Aldersgate, at Hosier Lane at about ten o'clock. A coach was waiting outside the house and, finding that there were already three gentlemen with the girl, they sent in one of their number, whereupon two of the earlier party withdrew,

4. 'David Garrick as the Farmer' in Garrick's *The Farmer's Return from London*, 1762, by Johann Zoffany

to the sound of scratching. He managed to put only two of the customary questions ('Were you poisoned?' — One knock; 'Can I procure you justice?' — One knock) before the rest of the company came in and the knocking ceased.

One of the gentlemen in the party, starting to put into operation the scheme already decided upon, placed himself by the bed, leaning against it; whereupon one of the Ghost's sympathizers requested him not to sit in that posture. 'Sir, I came here with a design to know the truth of this affair,' he rejoined heatedly, 'and I think I have a right to place myself in any part of the room, which I look upon as most suspicious.'

After further altercation and bad temper, the Ghost's sympathizers left in umbrage, and the gentleman by the bed offered to put Elizabeth up in a room at his house, to allow her the services of a maid and the attendance of anyone that Parsons chose, in order to further the investigation. Parsons turned down the offer. The gentleman then let it be known that he had the authority to say that 'if anything material happened, a person of distinction would interest himself in obtaining a discovery of this intricate affair'. Whether a threat or an inducement, the statement left Parsons unmoved.

The men sat until midnight, but the Ghost refused to knock. As they were leaving one of them noticed that the child was extraordinarily agitated and called attention to it. Someone else remarked: 'That it was because she [meaning the knocker] had not been entertained.'

The child was now frequently in strong convulsions, a return of the fits from which she had suffered earlier, in 1760, according to Mr. Gammon, the apothecary, and these, whether simulated or not, and so often associated with genuine psychical manifestations, deeply affected many of the auditors and led them to believe in the truth of the Ghost. As the correspondent who reported on this particular seance in the *London Chronicle* observed, the child's agitations 'move pity more than suspicions'.

Another member of the party asked the child if she had ever seen the Ghost and knew her?

> 'Yes.'
> 'Were you frightened at the sight?'
> 'No.'
> 'In what form or shape did she appear?'
> 'In a shroud, and without hands.'
> 'What! did this sight not frighten you?'
> 'No.'

On this inclusive note they left, but several others sat up with the girl all night and were rewarded at a quarter past seven in the morning by the Ghost beginning to scratch, but 'very low'. The child, 'who had been composed the former part of the night', was asked if she would persuade Fanny to respond louder: 'She complied, but faintly.' A number of questions were then put, to try her consistency and test her knowledge of Fanny Lynes's biography, but some were new.

> 'Do you know what the poison was?' — One knock.
> 'Was it arsenic?' — One knock.
> 'Did Mr. Kent ever hurt you by pinching?' — One knock.
> 'Do you desire him to be hanged?' — One knock.
> 'Shall you then be at rest?' — One knock.
> 'Are you willing that your corpse should be taken up?' — One knock.
> 'Can the poison be discovered?' — One knock.
> 'Is Mr. Kent willing that it should be taken up?' — Two knocks.
> 'Is Mr. Kent now married?' — One knock.
> 'Is Mrs. Kent with child?' — One knock.
> 'Is she uneasy?' — One knock.
> 'Would you have the clergyman insist upon the taking up your body?' — One knock.

The answers were those that could have been expected and contained nothing new, but the circular dialogue was proceeding gradually to draw attention to Frances Lynes's body in the vaults of St. John's.

When Fanny had gone, James Penn of St. Ann's turned to Parsons and said: 'Mr. Parsons, for the satisfaction of the public, and to put an end to the present distress of your own family, and also of that of Mr. Kent, will you give your consent to the removal of the child to Mr. Aldrich's house?' Parsons agreed and when Elizabeth herself was asked for her consent she agreed as freely.

The scheme devised was that Elizabeth should be taken to Aldrich's house and put to bed in a bed standing by itself in the middle of a large empty room, and chairs were to be placed round it. No one hitherto connected with her was to be allowed in the room, not even her father. She was to be properly examined, in the presence of some of the clergy, a physician, a surgeon, an apothecary, and a justice of the peace; and other gentlemen of reputation, both clergy and laity, were also to be asked to attend. Having secured Parsons's consent and agreed with him that the trial should be held on Friday evening, January 22, Penn left to make arrangements.

The writer of the account of this seance printed in the *London Chronicle* was greatly distressed by the night's happenings. 'What must occasion incredulity is', he concluded, mentioning one of the saddest and more horrifying aspects of the affair, 'the afflicting an innocent child, whom this spirit acknowledges so to be, and that it is not the part of a good spirit so to do, which she knocks that she is, and permitted by God, not by Satan, to appear. What's more astonishing, that she will not cease troubling the child after satisfaction had. There is such a mixture of truth and contradictions, that a person cannot help doubting of the veracity of this knocker. It is, we humbly presume, fit to be enquired into, for the satisfaction of the Public, and to bring to exemplary punishment the impostor, or impostors, if any, to relieve a distressed family, to preserve the reputation of the innocent, or to vindicate the cause of the injured.'

The plan to examine the girl at Aldrich's house received, however, a sudden check. When James Penn, in company with a gentleman of 'veracity and fortune' and his sister, called on Parsons on the Friday morning, he asked them very roughly what they wanted?

'Is the child here?' Penn enquired.
'No.'
'Where is she?'
'I shall not tell you. She shall go no where, nor be seen any more.'
'Did not you and the girl both consent to go to Aldrich's house?' Penn demanded.
'No matter for that; she shall go no where.'

Parsons had clearly been consulting his friends in the interval, and further evidence of these consultations appeared immediately in the *Public Ledger*.[1] An account was published, supposedly drawn up as long ago as February 25, 1760, and signed 'J. A. L.', pretending to tell how 'an intimate friend' of William Kent's had 'very dextrously' brought Fanny Lynes up from Norfolk to East Greenwich, a journey of a hundred miles in a day, on Kent's instructions. At the right moment Kent's friend ('who had some small knowledge of the law!') drew up a will for Fanny in Kent's favour. The places they had lived in after leaving Greenwich were described. No charges were made, but the tone was menacing: all

[1] I am assuming that these communications first appeared in the *Ledger*; I have taken them from the *St. James Chronicle*, January 21–23, 1762.

things, J. A. L. observed, had had 'the desired effect'. To this narrative was added an appendix signed 'R. Browne, Amen Corner' and dated January 21, 1762, in which details of Fanny's death were brought to public notice. Browne asserted that Fanny's sister, Ann, who lived in Pall Mall, had heard of Fanny's illness on or about January 31, 1760, and had gone to see her. She found her ill, but 'in a fair way of doing well'. She sent the following day to find out how she did and learnt that she had had sufficient strength to have sat up in bed. The following morning she was told that she was dead, which had surprised her greatly. She had attended the funeral at St. John's, at Kent's request, but as the coffin was already screwed down, she had been denied 'the pleasure of seeing her dear sister's body'. She had gone to call on Browne after the funeral and had told him Fanny's history to account for there being no plate on the coffin, though admittedly 'a very handsome one'.

Kent claimed to know the identity of 'J. A. L.', who from his initials was clearly a member of the Lynes family, perhaps even Fanny's brother John himself; and Richard Browne was a family connection. Their communications kept up the pressure on Kent and came timely when Parsons was refusing to keep his word to let Elizabeth be examined at Aldrich's.

But Parsons did allow the girl to be transferred that night, Friday, January 22, to the house of the matron of St. Bartholomew's Hospital, the rendezvous being kept secret to save it from being besieged by the multitude. About twenty people attended and as nothing at all happened all night, they relieved their boredom by tucking into 'the dried beef and sound port' that had been provided. One or two of them became so troublesome in their cups that they had to be put out. At about six o'clock in the morning three scratches were heard, like the noise of a cat's claws drawn across a cane chair, and that was all, though the scratches coming spontaneously and suddenly 'a good deal struck the imagination of the auditors'. The girl appeared to be sound asleep. One of the company began to argue very strongly that the whole affair was an imposture. Shortly after Elizabeth woke in 'a violent fit of crying and tears' and when she was asked why by 'a gentleman of the first rank in the literary world', and being assured that no harm would come to her, she declared she was weeping for fear of what 'would become of her Daddy, who must needs be ruined and undone, if their matter should be supposed to be an imposture.'

'But I thought you were in a sound sleep when I was talking,' exclaimed the gentleman, who had declared for an imposture.

'Aye, but not so sound but that I could hear all you said,' Elizabeth blurted out tearfully.

The only authority who could properly enquire into what had become a public scandal was the Lord Mayor. He had already been approached. On Tuesday, January 19, the day that 'Carrots' had been taken before the Ghost, a Mr. Watson went to Alderman Gosling and, after explaining the situation and that it was likely to become more serious, begged him to interpose. Gosling refused to act alone, but he accompanied Watson and John Moore to the Lord Mayor and the Lord Mayor agreed to hear their case on Saturday, January 23. Kent began in the meantime to prepare a deposition of the relevant circumstances of his life to lay before him.

On the Saturday, as arranged, Alderman Gosling, John Moore and Parsons called upon the Lord Mayor, Sir Samuel Fludyer, and Moore and Parsons proceeded to tell him their experiences of and confidence in the Ghost. Whatever they might have hoped Sir Samuel would do, they quickly found that he 'did not choose to stir much' in the affair, whichever way he inclined, for it seemed to him 'somewhat like Canning's affair'. The recollection of Canning's affair was sufficient to make any eighteenth-century Lord Mayor of London pause for thought.

The two great cautionary impostors of the century were Elizabeth Canning and Mary Tofts, and their names became popularly linked with Fanny's from the moment that she started to scratch. 'Elizabeth Canning and the Rabbit-woman were modest impostors in comparison of this,' Horace Walpole exclaimed, 'which goes on without saving the least appearances.'

Mary Toft's imposture was the earlier and the more extravagant. She claimed in November 1726 to have given birth to a litter of rabbits, and after examination she was supported by no less an authority than Nathanael St. André, anatomist to George I's household. The deception convinced several other doctors and a great part of the general public, following St. André's lead, and the controversy that followed was fought with batteries of squibs and pamphlets. Tofts confessed to the imposture in early December, and several reputations, including pre-eminently St. André's, were lost. The Tofts affair proved again what needed no proof, that some people will believe anything, and take pleasure in keeping their credulity in shape by stretching it to the limit; but its moral was more strictly applicable to credulous doctors than to lord mayors.

How different was the affair of Elizabeth Canning. Hers was a cautionary tale especially for lord mayors, and it is small wonder that her name occurred to Sir

Samuel as he sat discussing the Cock Lane Ghost. As if to make sure that Canning's name should be fresh in everyone's minds at this time, it had been announced in the newspapers in November 1761 that 'The noted Mrs. Freeman, lately Betty Canning, was married at Philadelphia in the time of her transportation, and is come over to England to see her friends here.' More ominous still, on January 26, as the scenes in Cock Lane were moving to a climax, the death was announced of 'Mary Squires, the gipsey, well remembered in Elizabeth Canning's affair'.

Elizabeth Canning's story was exceedingly simple; so simple as to amount to nothing, and in that nothing lay the mystery. Bet Canning, a servant girl of eighteen, marked with the smallpox and though well set up not particularly attractive, disappeared on January 1, 1753. She was advertised for as missing, but remained a month undiscovered. At the end of January she suddenly reappeared at her mother's, worn out and bedraggled, with a strange story to tell. As she had been coming home in the evening of January 1 she had been set upon by two ruffians, she declared, who had robbed and beaten her, whereupon she had thrown a fit. When she had come to her senses she had found herself being marched along between them. At about four o'clock in the morning they had reached a house. Dragged inside she had been threatened by a woman with a knife, robbed of her stays, and locked in an empty room. She had been left there unattended for the month and had lived on a pitcher of water and a loaf of bread that had been left in the room, and a penny mince pie she had happened to have had in her pocket. All she had been able to see through the boarded up casement was the passing of the stage coaches to Hertford. At last she had determined to break out and, clambering through the window, she had made a successful escape and arrived home on foot in a woebegone condition.

A hue and cry at once went up with appeals for subscriptions to see justice done, and it having been wonderfully and almost immediately decided on the strength of Bet's thimbleful of facts that she had been confined in a bawdy house kept by Mother Wells at Enfield, she was carried there in a procession to identify her captors. She picked out Mary Squires, a gipsy, as the woman who had robbed her of her stays, and both Squires and Mother Wells were promptly apprehended. Their trial came on at the Old Bailey and on February 26 Mary Squires was sentenced to death for robbery and Mother Wells, as an accessory after the fact, was branded and handed down six months' imprisonment. The prosecution was immeasurably strengthened by the evidence of Virtue Hall, one of Mother Wells's girls. Virtue corroborated Bet's story in every detail.

But a good many people were extremely perplexed by the inconsistencies of the evidence offered at the trial; among them the Lord Mayor himself, Sir Crisp Gascoyne. Perplexity soon turned to the gravest suspicion. Sir Crisp set enquiries on foot which proved that Mary Squires and her son and daughter had been in Dorset at the time of Bet's supposed abduction and had been travelling leisurely on foot towards Enfield during the period of her disappearance. They had arrived at Mother Wells's shortly before Canning and her party of supporters had descended on the house. Virtue Hall now declared before the Lord Mayor that the evidence she had given before Henry Fielding, as magistrate at Bow Street, was false, and had been uttered under threat of an indictment for felony. Hall asserted that Squires had not been at Mother Wells when she was supposed to have robbed Canning, arriving some weeks later, and that Canning had never been seen at Mother Wells until the day she had appeared and lodged her charges. Other evidence was forthcoming to prove that the room Canning claimed she had been confined in had been occupied all the time by Fortune Natus and his wife, a couple of exemplary character.

The inconsistencies in Bet's story had already alienated some of her earliest supporters. They could not understand why her first description of her place of confinement tallied in scarcely a particular with the actual room in Mother Wells's; or how no one had happened to witness her wonderful ten miles' trek back to London, in an outward condition that could hardly have escaped notice: the midwife who had examined her for assault on her return had commented upon the remarkable cleanliness of her shift. And the more they thought the more incredible it began to seem that she could have survived for so long on so little. They were slow to grasp what Horace Walpole had appreciated at a glance. 'For my own part, I am not at all brought to believe her story, nor shall, till I hear that living seven-and-twenty days without eating,' he wrote, with his usual nonchalance, 'is among one of those secrets for doing impossibilities, which I suppose will be at last found out, and about the time that I am dead, even some art of living for ever.' Sir Crisp Gascoyne himself had been so disturbed by these inconsistencies as to set enquiries on foot, and on the strength of their evidence, he issued a warrant for Canning's arrest. Squires's execution was respited, and she was later given a free pardon.

Sir Crisp had acted with courage. At the time of Squires's and Wells's trial feelings had run so high in

favour of Canning that a mob had besieged the Court to
prevent those wishing to give evidence on behalf of the
accused from entering, and had treated them as though
they themselves were guilty. And when Sir Crisp had
initiated enquiries, he had been attacked with every
calumny and prejudice; suggestions were even made
that he himself had a secret interest in the matter; and
Canning's supporters obviously hoped he would fail to
incriminate her so that their confidence might be justi-
fied. The controversy raged in print. Henry Fielding
wrote in support of Canning and the opposite view was
argued more effectively by the officious journalist and
naturalist, John Hill, and by Allan Ramsay, the painter.

The pamphleteers had time enough to write and could
count upon interest being maintained, for such a com-
plex affair could not be concluded quickly. A bill against
Canning for perjury had first to be brought in and found
true, and not until April of the following year was she
brought up for trial at the Old Bailey. The trial lasted
for more than a week, with mobs and riots about the
sessions-house; and Sir Crisp was so insulted and abused
that 'the court of aldermen offered a reward for discovering any of the rioters'. The jury at first returned a verdict
of guilty, with a recommendation to mercy, and gave
further trouble before Canning could be sentenced, to
seven years' transportation to the American colonies.

The sentence was not the end of the affair. The evidence Sir Crisp had collected proved her guilty of perjury
and her victims innocent; but a mystery remained — and
is yet unsolved. Where was Elizabeth Canning for the
whole of January 1753, if she was not at Mother Wells's?
She was never proved to have been elsewhere. During
the long course of the investigation and the trial, not a
single witness stepped forward to claim that she had been

49

glimpsed somewhere in public, nor could her opponents offer more than plausible reasons for her disappearance — 'there are such distempers as lyings-in and miscarriages, to which young servant-maids of eighteen are very much subject', Allan Ramsay broadly hinted — or even conjecture as to her true whereabouts. Her evidence would not stand up to criticism, but there were facts in it that could not be explained away as fabrications. Many of her supporters remained convinced of her truth, and if their faith can be explained as self-conceit, Elizabeth Canning herself never betrayed what she had really been doing for the month. She continued to assert that she had been imprisoned at Mother Wells's.

Sir Crisp Gascoyne himself at the end of his term of office felt compelled to take the unusual step of publishing an address to the Liverymen of London on his conduct of the Canning case. He would have been prepared, he said, to have suffered in silence the 'many severe reflections' that he had had to endure, but he had thought it necessary to vindicate himself as a magistrate: 'It is not proper that the lord-mayor of London should be condemned where he is innocent', nor right that a blot should 'remain upon that year of the City's administration — a city, amongst its many other pre-eminent distinctions, at all times heretofore distinguished by the exemplary conduct of its magistrates'. After fully recounting the evidence which had led him to indict Canning for perjury, he ended by affirming, 'What I did as a man, my heart tells me was right; but as a magistrate, I readily submit to your judgment.'

As Sir Samuel Fludyer sat listening on January 23 to the account of the Cock Lane Ghost, he could not help but notice its disturbing similarities to the affair of Bet Canning. The element of mystery, the assumption of

guilt, the inspired reports in the newspapers, the seriousness of the charges levelled, the youth and apparent
innocence of the instruments, the pertinacity of the
accusers, the parties of rival supporters, the intense
popular interest, were the principal aspects shared in
common. As Sir Samuel ran through the list he would
glumly recognize that only one parallel had been omitted: his appointment to play the part earlier assigned to
Sir Crisp Gascoyne. Were that to happen he could look
forward to a year of obloquy and distress, at a time when
political passions themselves were threatening to run
higher than ever before, aroused by the idea of the in-
fluence of the King's Scotch favourite, Lord Bute. As the
Ghost seemed 'to the Lord Mayor somewhat like Canning's affair his Lordship did not choose to stir much in
it' — his sentiment could not have been more sincere.

He would not issue a warrant for the arrest of either
Kent or Parsons, on a charge of murder or conspiracy
respectively, as Sir Crisp had acted in the case of Canning — and only the Lord Mayor's warrant ran in the
City — but he gave directions that the scheme of enquiry
as proposed to be held at Stephen Aldrich's house should
be carried out, and ordered that neither trouble nor
expense should be spared in detecting the truth. By this
means, he might forestall the worst, and prevent himself from suffering Sir Crisp's uncomfortable fate.

The time to act was becoming almost overdue. The
fear induced by the Ghost was approaching hysteria
among the impressionable. The newspapers reported that
the injudicious trumpeting of the story had caused such
terror in a ladies' boarding school that the younger
children had been frightened to go up the stairs, or to
bed, or to sleep when they were coaxed to bed; and
similar terror reigned in private families. These reports

were far from exaggeration. In the parish of St. Sepulchre's, at 37 King Street, there was a well-known and
long-established ladies' charity school, to which Dr.
Johnson himself was a subscriber, and the ladies on the
committee had to censure the schoolmistress herself for
listening to stories of the Ghost and, according to the
minutes, to desire her 'to keep her belief in the article to
herself'. And in the meantime, the credulous and the
frivolous continued to mingle in crowds in Cock Lane.
'The clergy and laity, the nobility and commonalty,' the
newspapers announced, 'continue their nightly attendance upon the invisible agent. Nor are the ladies less
curious upon the present, than upon most other occasions; insomuch, that the narrow avenue of Cock-Lane
is become a sort of midnight rendezvous, occupied by a
string of coaches from one end to the other.'

In the evening of the same Saturday as the approach
to the Lord Mayor, Elizabeth was put to bed with 'a
gentlewoman of reputation', but nothing happened. On
the following Sunday, a more extended seance was held,
in a house opposite to the schoolhouse in Cock Lane.
The Reverend Mr. Ross, one of the two clergymen in
attendance, in company with Lord Dartmouth and 'an
eminent surgeon', tried to put the enquiry on an altogether higher plane than it had hitherto occupied and
to set the Ghost some philosophical questions, with the
idea of settling a long-disputed question, what kind of
vehicle do spirits inhabit?

> 'Are you clothed in a body?' Ross asked. — One knock.
> 'Are you clothed in a body of flesh?' — Two knocks.
> 'In a body of air?' — Two knocks.
> 'In a body of light?' — One knock.

He appears to have rested satisfied with this information,
which no doubt confirmed his own private speculation.

The surgeon made an examination, placing 'his hand upon the girl's stomach and other parts, whilst the answers were given, but this, as well as every other method hitherto thought of, has proved totally ineffectual'.

Stephen Aldrich and James Penn had meanwhile approached Parsons and told him of the Lord Mayor's determination that the child should be examined at Aldrich's house, in the manner already settled. Parsons consented to the examination, 'provided that some persons connected with the girl might be permitted to be there, to divert her in the day-time'. The request was disallowed as being contrary to the plan. He then suggested as Elizabeth's companion a woman known to be constantly with her, and, as an alternative, an equally unsuitable person, one who 'had disobliged her father, and was out at service'.

'Mr. Parsons,' Aldrich and Penn remonstrated, 'if you can procure any person or persons, of strict character and reputation, who are housekeepers, such will be with pleasure admitted.'

He asked for time to find such a person, but instead of returning himself, he sent an intermediary, William Lloyd, of Brook Street, Holborn, with a note to the effect that he must first consult his friends, who were not available, before consenting to the removal of the girl. Within three hours, he sent a further note by the same emissary, agreeing to Elizabeth's examination at Aldrich's, depending on the Lord Mayor's approbation, which, as he well knew, had already been given.

The strain of bargaining, added to the fatigue of excitement and sleeplessness was beginning to prove too much for Parsons, and on Monday, January 25, he asked that his house should be free from company for the one night.

Parsons was proving a very tricky customer and in order to bring matters to a head, Aldrich and Penn issued an account of their negotiations with him. He immediately riposted with an announcement in the *Public Ledger* for Tuesday, January 26: 'Whereas several advertisements have appeared in the papers reflecting upon my character, who am father of the child which now engrosses the talk of the town; I do hereby declare publicly, that I have always been willing and am now ready to deliver up my child for trial into the hands of any number of candid and reasonable men, requiring only *such security* for a fair and gentle treatment of my child, as no father of children or man of candour would refuse.'

The statement was not uncleverly phrased with an eye to arousing sympathy and Aldrich and Penn felt compelled to reprint it in *Lloyd's Evening Post*, for January 25–27, with the following comment: 'We are greatly puzzled to find Mr. Parsons asserting', they wrote, 'that he hath been *always* willing *to deliver up* the child, when he refused a gentleman on Wednesday evening the 20th inst. and even denied to us, that he had given his consent to Mr. Penn. We assured him, that his child *should be treated* with the utmost care and tenderness: to satisfy him of which we proposed, that a person, or persons of character and reputation, housekeepers, of his own appointment, should be admitted to attend the child, provided that they had never been present, when any questions were proposed, and told him, that some gentleman, of whom he had a great opinion, would be there, but no such persons, as he recommended, who were highly exceptionable *to all candid and reasonable men*. What is to be understood,' they finally asked, in a postscript, 'by requiring security'?

5. 'English Credulity, or the Invisible Ghost', 1762

*British Museum*

In the face of such attacks, the Ghost's sympathizers
fought hard themselves to prove that there was no possible evidence of a cheat. The child was carried on
January 26 to the house of Jane Armstrong in the neighbourhood and spent the night suspended in a hammock.
The noises went on unabated and Mrs. Armstrong and
the rest of the audience were strengthened in their conviction that they were preternatural.

What with Mr. Ross's deep questions and the squibs
and paragraphs in the papers and the spectacle of the
child slung in a hammock, the Ghost became increasingly the rage: 'it is as much the mode to visit the ghost, as
the Prince of Mecklemberg' (the Queen's brother, just
arrived from Germany), wrote Horace Walpole, on
January 29, announcing that he was going himself on
Saturday, the following day.

> I could send you volumes on the ghost [he wrote to George
> Montagu]; I went to hear it — for it is not an *apparition*, but
> an *audition*. — We set out from the Opera, changed our
> clothes at Northumberland House, the Duke of York, Lady
> Northumberland, Lady Mary Coke, Lord Hertford, and I,
> all in one hackney coach, and drove to the spot; it rained
> torrents; yet the lane was full of mob, and the house so full
> we could not get in — at last they discovered it was the Duke
> of York, and the company squeezed themselves into one
> another's pockets to make room for us. The house, which is
> borrowed, and to which the ghost has adjourned, is wretchedly
> small and miserable; when we opened the chamber, in which
> were fifty people, with no light but one tallow candle at the
> end, we tumbled over the bed of the child to whom the ghost
> comes, and whom they are murdering there by inches in such
> insufferable heat and stench. At the top of the room are ropes
> to dry clothes — I asked, if we were to have rope dancing
> between the acts? — we had nothing; they told us, as they
> would at a puppet-show, that it would not come that night
> till seven in the morning — that is, when there are only

prentices and old women. We stayed, however, till half an hour after one.

When the *Public Advertiser* reported this visit of the nobility and their disappointment, it observed cynically that 'the noise is now generally deferred till seven in the morning, it being necessary to vary the time, that the imposition may be the better carried on'.

Stephen Aldrich, having secured the reluctant Parsons, had in the meantime been pushing ahead with the arrangements to put his plan into effect. The child was to be undressed and put to bed by trustworthy women at his house; her behaviour was to be closely observed while the spirit was knocking by a committee of reputable men drawn from several professions; and, when they had satisfied themselves as far as they could, the Ghost was to be required to fulfil a promise she had already made to Kent and repeated on several occasions to John Moore. She was to be asked to accompany Kent into the vaults of St. John's, Clerkenwell, and signify her presence there by knocking on Frances Lynes's coffin, the most striking indictment a Ghost of limited expression could possibly compass. The time and place of the investigation were not divulged to the public, 'for obvious reasons', as the newspapers announced.

Aldrich drew up his committee in consultation with Lord Dartmouth. They chose Mrs. Oakes, the matron of the Lying-in Hospital in Brownlow Street, to act as principal lady-in-waiting. They very wisely invited Dr. John Douglas, the shrewdest exposer of impostors, to act as one of their chief investigators. Among the examples of Douglas's detective skill, the unmasking of the Scotsman, William Lauder, was the most striking. Lauder attempted by forgery to prove that Milton was guilty of plagiarism, and persuaded no less a person than Dr. Johnson to write a preface and a postscript to the pamphlet in which he collected and published his proofs in 1750. Douglas showed conclusively that Lauder was a villain, but he was careful at the same time to exonerate Johnson from any share of guilt. Douglas's triumphs were well and pleasantly summed up by Oliver Goldsmith in *Retaliation*:

> Here Douglas retires from his toils to relax,
> The scourge of impostors, the terror of quacks . . .

The Ghost promised him scope enough for his talents.

Aldrich and Lord Dartmouth were puzzled at first to choose a doctor, but they decided to invite Dr. George Macaulay, a well-known physician and husband of Catherine Macaulay, who was in a few years to become famous as a Whig historian. Another member of the committee was a Captain Wilkinson, but he appears to have selected himself. He was so determined to uncover the Ghost that he had already forced himself into one of the more select seances with a loaded pistol in his pocket and carrying a stick. The pistol was for firing into wherever the knocking seemed to come from and the stick for securing his retreat. Luckily for everyone, the Ghost had resolved not to sound that night; the best proof so far of her ghostly discretion. Wilkinson must have been hard to refuse a place. James Penn, Aldrich's confederate, was also a member, and John Moore another.

The most prominent of the committee was Samuel Johnson.

# V

## THE CLERKENWELL PYRAMID

WHEN Rasselas, Prince of Abyssinia, with his sister, the Princess Nekayah, Pekuah, her attendant, and Imlac, the poet, left the Happy Valley to travel abroad in Egypt and experience life under the ordinary dispensation, the companions visited a pyramid. Imlac indicated to them the principles of its construction, which had allowed it to survive earthquakes. 'A concussion that should shatter the Pyramid would threaten the dissolution of the continent', he observed.

The party went on to explore the interior of this ancient wonder, but as they were about to enter, Pekuah drew back, startled and a-tremble. 'Pekuah,' said the princess, 'of what art thou afraid?' 'Of the narrow entrance,' answered the lady, 'and of the dreadful gloom. I dare not enter a place which must surely be inhabited by unquiet souls. The original possessors of these dreadful vaults will start up before us, and perhaps shut us in for ever.' She broke off and threw her arms round the neck of her mistress.

'If all your fear be of apparitions,' said the prince, 'I will promise you safety: there is no danger from the dead: he that is once buried will be seen no more.'

'That the dead are seen no more,' said Imlac, 'I will not undertake to maintain against the concurrent and unvaried

58

testimony of all ages, and of all nations. There is no people, rude or learned, among whom apparitions of the dead are not related and believed. This opinion, which, perhaps, prevails as far as human nature is diffused, could become universal only by its truth: those that never heard of one another would not have agreed in a tale which nothing but experience can make credible. That it is doubted by single cavillers, can very little weaken the general evidence; and some who deny it with their tongues confess it by their fears.

'Yet I do not mean to add new terrors to those which have already seized upon Pekuah. There can be no reason why spectres should haunt the Pyramid more than other places, or why they should have the power or will to hurt innocence and purity.'

Thus spoke Johnson, imagining himself in the shade of the pyramids; the confident solemn tones of Imlac, his mouthpiece, rebuking Rasselas for his doubt. In this instance, as in so many others, he appeals for support of his opinion to the general sense of mankind, and relies on it for his belief that the dead can return, proving by their appearance that there is life after death. The discussion between Imlac and Rasselas is written with all his customary sense of responsibility: those who hold with Rasselas are asked to consider how small a minority they belong to among the races and generations of men; and those who already believe will find their belief strengthened by being so roundly confirmed. And the tenderness he could feel is shown, too, in his determination that anyone who religiously accepted the truth of spirits had no grounds for fear.

But when Johnson was no longer Imlac travelling the Egyptian sands, but Samuel Johnson, a private citizen, strolling the familiar length of the Strand, he spoke differently. Pondering the authority which Imlac had invoked to rout Rasselas's disbelief, that man had always and everywhere expressed a belief in ghosts, he was no longer satisfied. The belief was common, indeed, but on what was it based? 'It is wonderful,' he observed to Boswell, 'that five thousand years have now elapsed since the creation of the world, and still it is undecided whether or not there has ever been an instance of the spirit of any person appearing after death. All argument is against it; but all belief is for it.'

A belief in ghosts was a religious requirement. Christianity or any other religion that preached the survival of the soul after death had to believe that the spirits of the departed could on occasion and under divine dispensation manifest themselves; and every instance of their appearance, as well as other discoveries of the occult, was cherished for the sake of the support it offered to men's faith in the realm of spirits. After 1660 in England, when the foundation of the Royal Society can be taken as symbolizing the rising authority of science, the entire classification of the occult and spiritualistic as superstition, and their rejection in accordance with Francis Bacon's saying that 'superstition is the reproach of the Deity', could be the first step towards atheism. Joseph Glanvill, defending a belief in witchcraft, remarked in *Saducismus Triumphatus*, published in 1681, on the advances atheism and infidelity had made and how dangerous they had become. 'Particularly the distinction of the Soul from the Body,' he continued, 'the being of spirits, and a future life are assertions extremely despised and opposed by men of this sort, and if we lose those articles, all religion comes to nothing.'

Johnson held the same view as Glanvill. The Christian truths were so important, since nothing less than man's eternal salvation depended on them, that everything must be done to prevent belief in Glanvill's articles from being challenged. Johnson could not fall under the charge directed against the Methodists, of actually encouraging credulity and superstition, but he did believe that the spirits of the dead could return and, with authority of the Church, that they could protect and counsel. When his dearly loved wife, Tetty, died in 1752 Johnson was plunged into profound gloom. 'I have ever since seemed to myself broken off from mankind,' he wrote to Thomas Warton, 'a kind of solitary wanderer in the wild of life, without any direction, or fixed point of view: a gloomy gazer on a world to which I have little relation.' And from these depths he prayed to God that if the souls of the dead were ordained to minister to the living, he might enjoy 'the good effects' of Tetty's 'attention and ministration, whether exercised by appearance, impulses, dreams, or in any other manner agreeable to thy Government'.

But Johnson's anxiety to believe in spirits extended beyond a defence of the articles of Christian faith to the reality of the after-life itself. He was so appalled by the idea of death that though he could depict Rasselas and his friends roaming with philosophic calm among the Catacombs, where the bodies were 'laid in rows on either side', when he came upon human bones himself, lying unburied in a ruined chapel on Raasay, he could not bear even to look at them. 'He started back from them with a striking appearance of horror.' He did not react so strongly to such remains because he was squeamish. Their horror consisted in showing how small a thing was man and to what ignominious shreds he must be reduced. They brought the idea of personal annihilation irresistibly to mind.

As a Christian, Johnson had to believe that death was followed by judgment and that eternal damnation was a

punishment God might inflict; a prospect so alarming
that he was once prompted to speak with such vehemence
on the theme as to compel gentle Mrs. Adams to ad-
monish him. 'You seem, sir, to forget', she said, 'the
merits of our Redeemer.' 'Madam,' he burst out in reply,
'I do not forget the merits of my Redeemer; but my
Redeemer has said that he will set some on his right hand
and some on his left.' — He was in gloomy agitation and
said, 'I'll have no more on't.' But more appalling than
damnation — of being sent to Hell 'and punished ever-
lastingly', as he simply and unflinchingly put it — was
annihilation, the mocking import of those pathetic
bones. Damnation depended upon the spirit persisting
on to receive its deserts, but annihilation meant a vacant
future, an idea from which Johnson passionately re-
coiled. 'There is one mode of the fear of death', Miss
Seward once remarked to him, 'which is certainly
absurd; and that is the dread of annihilation, which is
only a pleasing sleep without a dream.' All the time of
the discussion, into which he had been drawn, fascinated
against his will, Johnson had been 'standing upon the
hearth rolling about, with a serious, solemn, and somewhat gloomy air'. 'It is neither pleasing, nor sleep,' he
now observed, almost to himself; 'it is nothing. Now
mere existence is so much better than nothing, that one
would rather exist even in pain, than not exist. . . . The
lady confounds annihilation, which is nothing, with the
apprehension of it, which is dreadful. It is in the apprehension of it that the horror of annihilation consists.'

Religion required proofs of the spiritual to defend
itself against atheism, and were they forthcoming these
proofs would simultaneously dispel the fear of personal
annihilation. But where were these proofs? As Johnson
admitted, five thousand years of belief in spirits had pro-

duced no evidence of their reality. He himself had only had one experience of the preternatural. One day, as a student at Oxford, when he had been about to open his room, with the key in the lock, he had heard his mother, who was at Lichfield, 'distinctly call *Sam*'. He was under no doubt that his mother's voice had spoken, and being *called* is a sufficiently common phenomenon for him to have found corroborative evidence. Unfortunately, the *calling* was not followed by any consequences; he had been mysteriously hailed to no purpose. He himself never met with an apparition, though it would have been a glad confrontation, and in the long course of his enquiries, he came upon only one honest and sensible man who claimed to have seen one, and that was his old friend and original publisher, Edward Cave, of the *Gentleman's Magazine*, who had his offices in St. John's Gate, a short step from St. John's Church, Clerkenwell. Cave was unwilling to talk about his experience and seemed frightened if it was mentioned, but when pressed for a description of what he saw he could only call it 'something of a shadowy thing'. What could be less conclusive? And the appearance had again been to no effect.

Johnson himself wanted dearly to believe, but he was not credulous; whatever transpired in the irrational depths of his mind as he swayed gloomily to and fro, when he spoke he brought to bear the force of a reason undeceived. He knew perfectly well that the imagination could play tricks. He drew a clear distinction between what *is* and what *seems* in one of his many discussions of the occult with Boswell, who delighted to raise the subject.

> Sir [he explained], I make a distinction between what a man may experience by the mere strength of his imagination, and what imagination cannot possibly produce. Thus, suppose I should think that I saw a form, and heard a voice

cry 'Johnson, you are a very wicked fellow, and unless you repent you will certainly be punished'; my own unworthiness is so deeply impressed upon my mind, that I might *imagine* I thus saw and heard, and therefore I should not believe that an external communication had been made to me.

On these grounds any apparition or other occult happening could be put down to imagination on the part of the perceiver and to delusion, if others accepted what they were told. And even if such a phenomenon was in fact genuine, it could not be proved to be so, except under one condition, which Johnson proceeded to explain. 'But if a form', he went on, 'should appear, and a voice should tell me that a particular man had died at a particular place, and a particular hour, a fact which I had no apprehension of, nor any means of knowing, and this fact, with all its circumstances, should afterwards be unquestionably proved, I should, in that case, be persuaded that I had supernatural intelligence imparted to me.'

Johnson made his criteria of judgment perfectly clear in these remarks, which indeed he repeated on other occasions, and how he proposed to apply them was demonstrated in his Life of Roscommon. When Wentworth Dillon — later Earl of Roscommon — was a boy, John Aubrey tells us that he was one day 'as it were, madly extravagant in playing, leaping, getting over the tables, boards, etc. He was wont to be sober enough; they said, "God grant this bodes no ill-luck to him!" In the heat of this extravagant fit, he cries out, "My father is dead!" A fortnight after, news came from Ireland, that his father was dead.' The story exactly satisfied Johnson's requirement: something was told that could have been learnt only by preternatural means: and after quoting it from Aubrey, Johnson proceeded to stress its significance:

The present age is very little inclined to favour any accounts of this kind, nor will the name of Aubrey much recommend it to credit: it ought not, however, to be omitted, because better evidence of a fact cannot easily be found than is here offered; and it must be by preserving such relations, that we may at last judge how much they are to be regarded. If we stay to examine this account, we shall see difficulties on both sides; here is a relation of a fact given by a man who had no interest to deceive, and who could not be deceived himself; and here is, on the other hand, a miracle which produces no effect; the order of nature is interrupted, to discover not a future but only a distant event, the knowledge of which is of no use to him to whom it is revealed. Between these difficulties, what way shall be found? Is reason or testimony to be rejected? I believe what Osborne says of an appearance of sanctity may be applied to such impulses or anticipations as this: 'Do not wholly slight them, because they may be true; but do not easily trust them, because they may be false.'

Roscommon's intuitive perception of his father's death was one instance of the preternatural which satisfied Johnson's requirements, but though he searched for others to add to it, he met with none until late in life. In 1789 Lord Lyttelton, known as 'the wicked Lord Lyttelton', both as a sign of his notorious profligacy and to distinguish him from the other Lord Lyttelton, the poet and friend of poets, and a Methodist sympathizer, died. Three days before his death he came down in the morning with a violent headache and rather upset, and told them he had had a very remarkable dream,

which he said would have made a deep impression on his mind, had he been possessed of even the least particle of superstition:— He had started up from a midnight sleep, on perceiving a bird flirting near the bed curtains, which vanished shortly, when a female spectre, in white raiment, presented herself, and charged him to depend on his dissolution in three days; he lamented jocosely the shortness of the warning, and observed it was too short a time for preparation after so disorderly a life.

The dream happening on a Wednesday night, he was well enough on the Saturday to go to Epsom and he remarked facetiously to a friend that he would soon 'jockey the ghost', the third day being almost up. He took a stroke and expired as he was getting into bed that very night. Such was the story that appeared in the newspapers immediately after his death, the details all vouched for on the evidence of friends. As a final touch, on the night of his death, November 27, a friend of his dreamed that Lyttelton's ghost appeared by his bedside, drew back the curtains, and said, ' "My dear friend, it is all over; you see me for the last time": or words to that effect.'

Johnson's conditions were again met. Here was information, of the direst import, that could be gained in no way other than the preternatural; and, on this occasion, the medium was not a wandering voice 'but an actual spirit'. Johnson was greatly comforted by it.

> 'It is the most extraordinary thing that has happened in my day,' he said; 'I heard it with my own ears, from his uncle, Lord Westcote. I am so glad to have every evidence of the spiritual world, that I am willing to believe it.' 'You have evidence enough,' Dr. Adams mildly rebuked him; 'good evidence, which needs not such support.' 'I like to have more,' Johnson rejoined, doggedly.

Johnson's tones are one of the voices of the century, solemn and disturbed. Another can be heard in the sceptical mockery with which Walpole greeted the account of Lyttelton's visitation; the same voice that had commented so wittily years before on the Cock Lane Ghost. 'If you can send us any stories of ghosts out of the north, they will be very welcome,' he wrote to William Mason in Yorkshire, 'Lord Lyttelton's vision has revived the taste; though it seems a little odd that an apparition should despair of being able to get access to his Lordship's bed in the shape of a young woman, without being forced to use the disguise of a robin redbreast.'

Johnson had only read about Roscommon's occult intelligence and was to hear of Lyttelton's ghostly intimation, but the Cock Lane Ghost happened a few minutes' walk away. All he had to do was to clap his hat on his head and call on it. As a spirit, Fanny met all the stringent conditions that Johnson had laid down. She purported to tell what had been hidden from even her medical attendants: that she had been poisoned. Were this to be verified, the spiritual world would have been sensationally vindicated. But not only would the existence of spirits have been demonstrated, and their power to manifest themselves when the occasion required; they would have shown their interest in maintaining moral stability by Fanny's bringing her murderer to book. Spirits had always been feigned as agents of retribution, but they had seldom been actually caught in the act. Johnson was deeply aware of Fanny's unique interest and significance, and even had he not joined the investigating committee he would certainly have followed the seances closely and looked forward to their result.

When Sir John Hawkins mentioned the Cock Lane Ghost affair in his Life of Johnson, he strongly implied that Johnson's interest was no better than superstitious and that by it he gave countenance to the credulity of the vulgar. Boswell properly took issue with Hawkins and others of the same view when he came to the Ghost in his own biography, where he stressed that Johnson's interest was 'philosophical', as, in the broader sense of the word, it can be shown to be. But even Boswell's account leaves a suspicion that Johnson was somewhat 'weakly credulous' in the matter, and this is hardly surprising since, as Edmond Malone shrewdly pointed out, Boswell himself was so enamoured of 'the mysterious' that he was constantly inveigling Johnson into discussing such matters, all of which he reported of course in his biography.

Johnson's interest in the Ghost as a manifestation of spirit was indeed deep, but there were additional reasons. If the Ghost was an imposture then it was of the worst kind, one that brought the spiritual into disrepute by exposing it to the coarsest ridicule and thereby undermining the reverence essential to religion. The infidel would be encouraged by a pantomime mounted by clerical fools, and the Christian depressed by evidence that the devout were short of reason. In this case, the Ghost ought to be suppressed as soon as possible in the interests of decency and public quiet, but only an investigation and test of its falsehood could bring that about.

The last consideration that led Johnson to join in questioning the Ghost was probably the immediate spur to his taking action. Fanny had returned to earth that justice might be done, but if the Ghost was 'a lying spirit', as Kent had charged, or if it was an imposition and not a spirit at all, with human knuckles doing the work attributed to ghostly vibrations, then the injustice was flagrant, with Kent and not Fanny as the victim. Harassed in mind beyond belief, by having his private life and his past a matter of common gossip, accused of the most scandalous crime by an agent whom he was utterly unable to confront, his domestic peace in jeopardy, and no end in sight to a persecution that could not be held accountable for its charges; was ever a man more miserably situated? Were it for no other reason than to terminate Kent's anxieties, Johnson would have wanted to examine the Ghost. If superstition was marked in his character, charity ran deeper, and Kent's predicament as a man would have moved him to action sooner than the lure of a ghost.

# VI

## 'SPEAK TO IT, HORATIO'

JOHNSON agreed to serve on the committee investigating
the Ghost as soon as he was approached, but at least one
of his friends, Saunders Welch, the magistrate, begged
him not to have anything to do with it. He would be
sure to be ridiculed, Welch argued, the argument likely
to have influenced Johnson least.

Stephen Aldrich had arranged for the examination
to take place at his house on Monday evening, February 1,
and in the morning he sent a note round to Dr. Douglas.

> The appointment for the examination stands [he wrote],
> as it did when I saw you last, viz. between 8 and 9 this
> evening. Mr. Johnson was applied to by a friend of mine
> soon after you left him, and promised to be with us: should
> be glad, if convenient, you'd show him the way hither. Mrs.
> Oakes, of Dr. Macauley's recommendation, I should be glad
> to have here on the occasion; and think it would do honour
> to the list of examiners to have Dr. Macauley with us.

The party assembled at Aldrich's as arranged. The
girl was examined and put to bed and the party waited
for the Ghost to manifest itself by knocking. Fanny was
then told that she would now be held to her promise of
accompanying Kent into the vault of St. John's and
rapping on her coffin. At the end of the investigation
Johnson was asked to draw up a report of the evening's
proceedings, which was read and approved by the other

## Cock-Lane, Humbug.

THE town it long has been in pain
  About the phantom in Cock-Lane,
To find it out they ſtrove in vain
  Not one thing they neglected ;
They ſearched the bed and room com-
To ſee if there was any chear,   (pleat.
While little Miſs that looks ſo ſweet,
  Was not the leaſt ſuſpected.

Then ſoon the knocking it begun
And then the ſcratching it wou'd come
'Twas pleaſed to anſwer any one,
  And that was done by knocking ;
If you was poiſon'd tell us true,
For yes knock one, for no knock two,
Then ſhe knock'd I tell to you,   (ing.
  Which needs muſt making it ſhock-

On Friday night as many know,
A noble Lord did thither go,
The Ghoſt its knocking wou'd not ſhow
  Which made the Gueſt to mutter :
They being gone then one was there
Who always called it my dear,
Fanny was pleas'd 'tis very clear,
  And then began to flutter.

The Ghoſt ſome Gentlemen did tell,
If they would go to Clerkenwell,
Into the Vault where ſhe did dwell,
  That they three knocks ſhould hear ſir
On Monday night away they went,
The man accus'd he was preſent,
But all as death it was ſilent,
  The de'll a knock was there ſir.

The Gentlemen return'd again,
And told young miſſy flat and plain,
She was the Agent of Cock-Lane,
  Who knock'd and ſcratch'd for Fanny
'Twas falſe each perſon did agree,
Miſs begg'd to go with her daddy
And then went into the Country
  To knock and ſcratch for Fanny.

6. Broadside Ballad: 'Cock-Lane,
Humbug', 1762

examiners before being sent to the newspapers for immediate publication.

Johnson's report was introduced by an attestation by Aldrich, meant to combat the rumours being deliberately circulated through the medium of the *Public Ledger* by the Ghost's promoters, who were trying to foster belief in the Ghost and to suggest that the investigating committee was biased. 'I think it proper to acquaint the Publick', Aldrich wrote, 'that the following account of the proceedings of the Committee of Gentlemen, who met at my house on Monday evening, in order to enquire into the reality of the supposed visitation of a departed Spirit at a house in Cock-lane, is alone authentic, and was drawn up, with the concurrence and approbation of the assembly, while they were present; and that the account in the *Ledger* of this day contains many circumstances not founded in truth'. Johnson's report followed.

> On this night many Gentlemen, eminent for their rank and character, were, by the invitation of the Rev. Mr. Aldrich of Clerkenwell, assembled at his house, for the examination of the noises supposed to be made by a departed spirit, for the detection of some enormous crime.
>
> About ten at night, the gentlemen met in the chamber, in which the girl, supposed to be disturbed by a spirit, had, with proper caution, been put to bed by several ladies. They sat rather more than an hour, and hearing nothing went downstairs, when they interrogated the father of the girl, who denied, in the strongest terms, any knowledge or belief of fraud.
>
> The supposed spirit had before publicly promised, by an affirmative knock, that it would attend one of the gentlemen into the vault, under the church of St. John, Clerkenwell, where the body is deposited, and give a token of her presence there by a knock upon her coffin: It was therefore determined to make this trial of the existence or veracity of the supposed spirit.

F

While they were enquiring and deliberating, they were summoned into the girl's chamber by some Ladies, who were near her bed, and who had heard knocks and scratches. When the gentlemen entered, the girl declared that she felt the spirit like a mouse, upon her back, and was required to hold her hands out of bed. From that time, though the spirit was very solemnly required to manifest its existence, by appearance, by impression, on the hand or body of any present, by scratches, knocks, or any other agency, no evidence of any preternatural power was exhibited.

The spirit was then very seriously advertised, that the person to whom the promise was made, of striking the coffin, was then about to visit the vault, and that the performance of the promise was then claimed. The company, at once, went into the church, and the gentleman, to whom the promise was made, went, with one more, into the vault. The spirit was solemnly required to perform its promise, but nothing more than silence ensued; the person supposed to be accused by the spirit, then went down, with several others, but no effect was perceived. Upon their return, they examined the girl, but could draw no confession from her. Between two and three she desired, and was permitted, to go home with her father.

It is therefore the opinion of the whole assembly, that the child has some art of making or counterfeiting particular noises, and that there is no agency of any higher cause.

What an illustration of the age of reason! The fashionable women, the men of reputation, the gullible clergy, the possessed child, the seriousness of the charges, the midnight descent to the vault, with the stacked coffins shadowily lit by the trembling flame of the lamp: the judiciousness of Johnson's prose cannot disguise the fantasy of the scene.

Johnson himself was now convinced that the Ghost was a deception; the spiritual world had failed to acquit itself once again, and according to Boswell the publication of his report in the newspapers 'undeceived the world'. Boswell attributed too much to the power of Johnson's prose and too little to the almost irresistible combination of credulity, pride, and superstition. An indication of what was yet to happen came immediately after the enquiry. John Moore was so cast down by the Ghost's failure to knock on the coffin that he told Kent he now believed it to be an impostor and would assist in discovering it, but when Kent pressed him 'to make an affidavit of what he knew as it was in his power to put a stop to the affair and clear up his character and reputation to the world, and not only so but also be a means of retrieving what he had suffered in his business', Moore began to hesitate and draw back. He reaffirmed his belief in the Ghost and asserted that, from the answers she had given, he was certain there was something to be discovered. And even if Kent had not murdered Fanny as the Ghost had charged, yet this visitation was plainly a judgment on him for having lived with her in sin.

Many other people were of Moore's opinion and, in spite of Johnson's account, held that the investigation had not been sufficiently thorough, especially since reports of a most extraordinary kind were being busily circulated. The girl stayed at a comb-maker's in Cow Lane on Wednesday, February 3, and in the morning when the knocking had begun, and the bell of Newgate Prison started to toll for a man about to be hanged, the comb-maker asked the Ghost whether anybody was about to be hanged? and whether a man or woman? He was knocked the correct answers. Later in the day two surprising events occurred; first a loose curtain ring spun rapidly and independently on its rod, and, later in the day, when Elizabeth was turning a piece of meat on the spit, knocking of such violence came from the wainscot above the chimney that they thought it 'would have broke it all to pieces'. But a more sinister event happened in the evening, when the girl was put to bed at her father's house and the compliant Ghost questioned. Among the questions asked, ran the rather puzzled account in the newspapers, 'one was, why she [Fanny] did not knock on her coffin when the gentleman went into the vault, agreeable to her promise? to which she answered (we suppose by proper questions being put) that it was not there: and if we are not misinformed, that it was taken away. — This may possibly lead to a further serious enquiry.'

Parsons plainly realized he was in a very serious position indeed. He had to prove the Ghost not an imposture — and for this purpose he voluntarily agreed with another set of self-appointed examiners that they should take the girl to their house and submit her to tests. At the first house, a gentleman's near the Strand, to which she was carried, on Sunday, February 7, nothing at all happened that day, but on Monday, after she had been searched and put to bed in the same room as the husband and wife, as it grew towards dawn the usual knockings and scratchings were heard. The husband rang the bell for a servant to bring a light, and carrying it over to where the child slept, he found her lying quite still. But as he watched an unaccountable whispering began.

'What are you whispering about?' his wife asked from bed.
'We're not whispering,' he replied; 'it's something else. I'm trying to understand what is being said.'

He never made out the meaning behind the voice, but he and his wife and the servant were prepared to swear to the whispering and that the child's lips never moved.

On Tuesday night the noises were again absent, but on Wednesday they broke out so violently that the household was terrified and asked for the girl to be moved. The disturbances continued for several days after she had left.

Elizabeth was then taken on Sunday, February 14th, to the house of a Mr. Missiter, near Covent Garden, and Missiter was plainly determined to carry the inquisition as far as he decently could. The first night a maid slept with the girl, but though she lay with her legs across her and holding her hands, the knockings went on. The following night, a bed was made up for her in the middle of the floor of a large room and Missiter and a friend slept in the room with her. The noises sounded, questions were put and punctually answered, and the friend declared 'the impulse was within less than six inches of his ear'. On Tuesday there were further noises; and on Wednesday when they were again sounding, Missiter's companion rose and seated himself from where he could watch the child. She lay well clear of the walls and any wooden object and seemed to rest motionless; the noises sounding to come all the time from a glass fixed against one side of the room. Upon waking her up and telling her to put her hands out of bed, the noises ceased.

Poor child! The following night her hands were tied, but she managed to slip one out of the sling, and there were noises. As a result she slept the next two nights in a kind of a hammock, spreadeagled out, with her hands and feet fastened with fillets. The knockings and scratchings held their peace. Elizabeth's ordeal was now nearly at an end. She was told she had only Sunday night, February 21, left to prove her innocence; unless the Ghost was heard, she and her father and mother would all be sent to Newgate. These threats were attended by results, as might have been expected. Missiter had set his servants to keep a constant watch on her through a peep hole and they saw the girl get out of bed and take from the chimney a piece of board about four by six inches used to set the tea kettle upon. Missiter and his friends thought it better at first to connive in the deception and when the knockings occurred they were taken seriously. The listeners noticed, however, and the point would not be lost on those determined to support the Ghost against all odds, that the questions put were answered 'in so different a sound, that it was very apparent this method of operating was a fresh contrivance.' Indeed, they went even further; they said 'that they immediately perceived that the sound was in the bed, and not in distant parts of the room as it used to be'. The child strenuously denied she had secreted a piece of wood, but when the bed was searched it was inevitably found.

These are the principal facts [ran the report published in the newspapers], since the father's submission of his child to a second examination. Lest the public should imagine this affair might have been sooner determined, it is proper to acquaint them that the gentlemen concerned, from the extreme shyness of the supposed invisible agent, had not the same opportunities of trial which were so long and frequent at its former place of residence. Of these facts the Public must judge [it continued, striving for objectivity], and particularly, whether the iniquitous disposition of the girl, or any terror of impending ruin on herself and family, had the greater share in producing the above-mentioned artifice. It is natural however to believe this fallacy discovers an extraordinary propensity in her to amuse the world with a juggle of her own; and to abuse the character of a gentleman, whom we cannot doubt of being entirely innocent of the crime laid to his charge.

The girl was allowed to go home to her friends on the Monday. The knockings had now ceased; the Ghost was almost laid.

Kent himself had meanwhile been taking steps to scotch the rumours still in circulation. On February 8 he had issued an affidavit signed by Dr. Thomas Cooper and James Jones, the apothecary, recounting their attendance on Frances Lynes during the course of her pregnancy, and at the time of her death from smallpox. They stressed particularly that she was almost incapable of swallowing for fifty hours before she died and that the little fluid she did take was administered only by one or other of them.

But Cooper's and Jones's affidavit, even though it followed so closely upon Johnson's report, was insufficient to stop the new story being put about that the removal of Fanny's body from the vault of St. John's accounted for the Ghost's failure to knock on her coffin. The only way to refute this allegation was for the coffin itself to be examined, and on Thursday, February 25, Kent, in company with Stephen Aldrich, the undertaker, the clerk, and the sexton to the parish, descended into the vault. The undertaker identified the coffin, which was the only one without a plate or inscription, and to remove any doubt, opened it before Kent; 'and a very awful shocking sight it was'.[1]

John Moore had managed to preserve his belief in Fanny through thick and thin, even though he had not actively patronized the Ghost since Stephen Aldrich's enquiry, but the final descent into the vault, and the sense of eminent retribution, was too much even for him, and on this same day, February 25, he issued his retraction:

In justice to the person, whose reputation has been attacked in a most gross manner, by the pretended Ghost in Cock-

---

[1] This evidence alone is sufficient to prove that the undecomposed corpse seen by J. W. Archer about the middle of the 19th century could not have been Fanny's.

lane; to check the credulity of the weak; to defeat the attempts of the malicious, and to prevent further imposition, on account of this absurd phenomenon, I do hereby certify, that though, from the several attendances on this occasion, I have not been able to point out, how, and in what manner, those knockings and scratchings, of the supposed Ghost, were *contrived, performed*, and *continued*; yet, that I am convinced, that those knockings and scratchings were the effects of some artful, wicked contrivance; and that I was, in a more especial manner, convinced of its being such, on the first of this month, when I attended with several persons of rank and character, who assembled at the Rev. Mr. Aldrich's, Clerkenwell, in order to examine into this iniquitous imposition upon the Public.

Since which time I have not seen the child, nor heard the noises; and think myself in duty bound to add, that the injured person (when present to hear himself accused by the pretended Ghost) has not, by his behaviour, given the least ground of suspicion, but has preserved that becoming steadfastness, which nothing, I am persuaded, but innocence could inspire.

Kent's reputation had been attacked from the beginning by means of the press and it was to the press that he now turned to exonerate himself. On about February 25, a pamphlet on the Ghost was published under the title of *The Mystery Revealed; Containing a Series of Transactions and Authentic Testimonials respecting the supposed Cock-Lane Ghost; which have been concealed from the Public.* The pamphlet is usually attributed to Oliver Goldsmith; at least a receipt exists, dated March 5 and signed by Goldsmith, for the sum of three guineas for a pamphlet respecting the Ghost, and only this one pamphlet would seem to answer. The publisher was William Bristow, of St. Paul's Churchyard, who, on his own later admission, was responsible for inserting into the *Public Ledger* the original list of questions put to the Ghost and her answers, which charged Kent with murder. Bristow had achieved some success in 1759 with a pamphlet on another notorious case, Eugene Aram's murder of Daniel Clark, and he no doubt hoped to repeat it. The epigraph to *The Mystery Revealed*, an apt quotation from Dryden —

> Since none the living dare implead,
> Arraign him in the person of the dead.—

showed that the writer was deeply sympathetic to Kent. He was very well briefed indeed as to the facts of his life. He began by giving the history of Kent's marriage to Elizabeth Lynes and his subsequent relations with Fanny. He described Fanny's death and told of the visit by her sister before the funeral, and proceeded to detail the Ghost's persecution and its exposure, printing the account by Johnson. Kent's case is put in the strongest possible light, but there is no abuse of his enemies, or of the impostors; indeed, the writer states: 'I would not wish, however, to turn the popular resentment upon any particular person, but I think it my duty to divert it somewhere from the guiltless.' He ended by referring his readers to an account by a seventeenth-century Protestant divine, Adrian Regenvolscius, of a ghost known as Zachary that deceived the whole of Poland for five years, let alone Regenvolscius. The parallel between Zachary and Fanny was close, but in one respect it would not hold: 'Zachary was believed to be a real ghost by a Protestant divine; but I fancy no Protestant divine can be found among us, so much the old woman, as to lend even a moment's assent to the ghost in Cock-lane.'

Whether Goldsmith wrote it or not *The Mystery Revealed* is persuasive and elegant and worthy of him. He ruefully acknowledged the astonishing interest in the Ghost when he admitted in the preface to his *Essays*, published in 1765, that the 'public was too strenuously employed with their own follies, to be assiduous in estimating mine; so that many of my best attempts in this way have fallen victims to the transient topic of the times; the Ghost in Cock-Lane, or the Seige of Ticonderoga'. He may have been hiding that he himself had cashed in on the public interest — though he was being paid for his time, not his sympathy, which, as the pamphlet shows, was sincere and spontaneous.

But a pamphlet, even if by Goldsmith, was not enough, and Kent now set the law in motion. The Reverend John Moore, John Parsons, Mrs. Parsons, Mary Frazer, and Richard James, a reputable tradesman, who had been responsible for the lying reports in the *Public Ledger*, were charged with conspiracy. Kent had been anxious not to proceed against Moore, a dupe rather than a knave, but he was told that 'it would ease the minds of the people'. Moore would also be an example to those tempted to start other ghosts; a necessary precaution, since even before the final inquisition of the girl had ended there were rumours of more apparitions. On February 9 a new knocking ghost was expected to perform in a house in Broad court, near Bow Street, Covent Garden, but blind Sir John Fielding, the Bow Street magistrate sent 'his compliments with an intimation, that it should not meet with that lenity the Cock-lane spirit did, but that it should knock hemp in Bridewell. On which the ghost, very discreetly, omitted the intended exhibition.'

The trial of the conspirators was arranged to take place on July 10 in the Court of King's Bench, Guildhall, before Lord Mansfield.

# VII

## AN ENTERTAINING SPRITE

UNTIL the Cock Lane Ghost was shown to be an imposture by Stephen Aldrich's committee, ridicule of the Ghost was fairly restrained, at least in public; the charges against Kent were grave, and there was widespread belief in the Ghost. One or two publishers tried to exploit this credulity; at least two new editions of *Drelincourt on Death* were published, for the sake of Defoe's startling account of the apparition of Mrs. Veal appended to it, and a popular sixpenny pamphlet on Fanny herself was published specifically for 'the conviction of the incredulous';[1] but most of them were anxious to combat superstition, by tracing its history. A 'clergyman' was first in the field with a *History of Ghosts, Spirits, or Spectres*,[2] and his pamphlet was quickly followed by another, with the resounding title of *Anti-Canidia: or, Superstition Detected and Exposed. In a Confutation of the vulgar Opinion concerning Witches, Spirits, Demons, Magick, Divination, Omens, Prognostications, Dreams, Augurys, Charms, Amulets, Incantations, Astrology, Oracles, &c.* The pamphlet was written

[1] The pamphlet seems to have disappeared, though there were at least two editions. It was printed for E. Cabe, 'at his Circulating Library in Ave-mary Lane', and sold at the pamphlet-shops and by news-carriers.

[2] I have not seen this pamphlet; it was advertised in the *Public Advertiser* for January 26.

by a self-confessed 'feeble hand', but it was prompted by a sincere 'sally of indignation at the contemptible *wonder* in Cock Lane, that has made so much *noise*', and trusted that it would strengthen '*rational* knowledge and wisdom, which will of course improve us in true religion'.

The history of past impostures was searched for examples of possession similar to Elizabeth Parsons's, in order to show that the public was again being imposed on. A clerical correspondent in the *London Chronicle*, in the course of some shrewd remarks disproving the Ghost on religious grounds, reminded his readers of the Boy of Bilsdon. The Boy, a youth of thirteen, charged Joan Cock with witchcraft and was so far believed that she was tried at the Stafford Assizes in 1620. He could feign deafness and blindness and maintained his pose through the most painful examination; he was also able to void and cast thread and needles and crooked pins. Joan Cock was acquitted and the boy was detected, but only with difficulty. The *St. James's Chronicle*, which made a speciality of the Ghost, reminded its readers of the case of Richard Hathaway, who, like the boy of Bilsdon, had fits and could vomit pins, and who charged Sarah Morduck with bewitching him in 1690.

Reginald Scott's *Discoverie of Witchcraft*, published in 1584 and written specifically to prevent the persecution of witches, was searched for similar evidence, and the newspapers reprinted from his pages the account of how the spirit of the lady of the Mayor of Orleans was supposed in 1534 to bring charges against her husband by knocking. The Salem witches of New England, at the end of the seventeenth century, were also remembered. And, of more provincial interest than these grand perturbing affairs, someone discovered the fraud of the groaning tree in the New Forest. The tree groaned, but

when it was cut down a hollow pipe was found under-
ground. The publican on whose land the tree stood
prudently decamped.

The majority of the spectators who crowded into Cock
Lane went to be entertained and pleasantly frightened,
and as soon as Fanny was exposed, the Ghost and its
sincere and pious believers were drenched with ridicule.
The theatres took immediate advantage of the affair by
reviving Addison's pleasant comedy of *The Drummer: or,
The Haunted House.* The plot — which as far as its
'ghostly' interest is concerned was based on the 'Drummer of Tedworth', the most famous of all poltergeists,
whose story had been told by Joseph Glanvill — bore
little relation to the Cock Lane Ghost, but there was at
least a 'drumming spirit' that hides behind the wainscoting, and some credulous servants; and the dialogue
occasionally could be applied with amusing effect to
events in Cock Lane:

> ' 'Tis a very hard thing to be a butler in a house, that's
> disturbed,' the butler exclaims as the curtain goes up; 'He
> made such a racket in the cellar last night, that I'm afraid
> he'll sour all the beer in my barrels.'

Even better, as the scene is set in a 'gothic' country
house, the 'ghost' can be blamed on country solitude:

> ' 'Tis the solitude of the country that creates these whim-
> sies,' the butler exclaims; 'there was never such a thing as a
> Ghost heard of at London, except in the play-house.' —

a joke certain to bring the house down.

*The Drummer* was presented first at Covent Garden on
January 28 with 'Gentleman' Smith playing Trueman;
Sarah Ward, Lady Trueman; the comedian, William
Shuter, Vellum; and Mrs. Pitt, Abigail. Drury Lane
revived the comedy the following night with a much

stronger company; Mrs. Pritchard, supreme in both comedy and tragedy, took Lady Trueman, and the incomparable Kitty Clive, Abigail; but John Beard, the manager of Covent Garden, shrewdly put on *The Beggar's Opera* as a rival attraction, with Charlotte Brent singing Polly. Beard had made Miss Brent 'his most powerful engine to demolish the success and humble the pride of Drury Lane', in his contest with David Garrick for popularity.

The comedy was introduced at Covent Garden after the Ghost's exposure by a new prologue, written and spoken by 'Gentleman' Smith, one of the most accomplished and favourite actors of the day. The piece was widely reprinted:

> If in this credulous, believing age,
> We bring a harmless Ghost upon the Stage,
> Some will perhaps conclude — in hopes of gain,
> We've lur'd the Knocking Spirit from Cock-lane;
> For all must know, she fled the dreadful spell,
> That threaten'd her so hard — at Clerkenwell.
> Hither she, then, might fly for liberty,
> To 'scape the dangers of the deep Red Sea.
> Yet no alliance with such ghosts is here,
> As are not free of speech, and won't appear.
> (But, sure, 'tis wonderful, a female sprite,
> That's still all day,— should hold her tongue at night,
> Few wives, I fear, this silent gift possess;
> Their husbands wish — they'd prattle somewhat less.)
> We'll prove the story of our Phantom true,
> And fairly bring him out to public view;
> Nay, make him speak like any modern blade,
> And gossip freely with my lady's maid;
> Nor keep you up all night to see his tricks,
> Ladies — our Ghost begins to walk at six;
> His martial music, and a soldier's air,
> We hope, will recommend him to the Fair.
> All dread of airy visions then subdue,

Nor start, nor tremble, if the lights turn blue.[1]
'Tho' with a Ghost our comedy is heighten'd,
Ladies, upon my word, you shan't be frighten'd:
Our's is a Ghost that's faithful, fond and true,
Made up of flesh and blood — as well as you:
Then every evening come, in crowds undaunted;
We never think this house is too much haunted.

The theatre could also take ready advantage of the Ghost by introducing it into pantomime. The pantomime running at the time at Covent Garden was the very successful *Apollo and Daphne*, and when the King and Queen went to see it on February 11, a new scene taking off the Ghost was added.

> Harlequin, after a good deal of scampering over the stage, with Pantaloon, &c. &c. at his heels, being pretty hard pressed, strikes the back scene with his hand, which opens, and discovers a bed with a child in it, upon which a knocking and scratching is heard. Harlequin after a pause, in order to give a little solemnity to the farce, puts on a broad brimmed hat and a band, and with pen and paper in hand seems very gravely taking the answers, which Miss Ghost is pleased to make to his supposed questions: upon this Pantaloon and the rest enter, and Mr. Harlequin seems mighty busy in acquainting him with the discoveries he has made.

The initiative lay with John Beard. Garrick was slow to take off the Ghost effectively, but when he did reply he did so with originality and genius. On March 20, after being announced well in advance, he himself played the lead in his new interlude, *The Farmer's Return*. The piece was simply a vehicle for Garrick's extraordinary powers of mimicry and how far he sank himself in the part can be seen in Hogarth's brilliant sketch of him, sitting four square, legs apart, pipe in hand, with a look of shrewd amusement on his weatherbeaten face.

[1] The last six lines were from the original prologue to *The Drummer*.

The farmer is discovered at the moment of his return home from London, being welcomed by his wife and children, a girl and two boys. As soon as he has settled himself down with a pipe and a can of ale, he begins to describe all he has seen, the busy streets, the Royal Family, the theatres — and the Ghost!

I ne'er went to *opras*! — I thought it too grand,
For *poor* folk to like what they don't understand.
The top joke of all, and what pleas'd me the moast,
Some wise ones and I sat up with a *ghoast*.
WIFE AND CHILDREN. A ghoast! [*Starting*]
FARMER. Yes, a ghoast!
WIFE. I shall swoond away, Love!
FARMER. Odzooks! — thou'rt as bad as thy betters above!
With her nails and her knuckles, she answer'd so noice!
For *yes* she knock'd *once*, and for *no* she knock'd *twoice*.
*I* ask'd her *one* thing —
WIFE. What thing?
FARMER. If yo', dame, was true?
WIFE. And the poor soul knock'd *one*.
FARMER. By the zounds, it was *two*.
WIFE. I'll not be abus'd, Jahn. [*Cries*]
FARMER. Come, prythee no croying,
The ghoast, among friends, was much giv'n to loying.
WIFE. I'll tear out her eyes —
FARMER. I thought, dame, of matching
Your neails against hers — for you're both good at scratching.
They may talk of the country, but, I say, in town,
Their throats are much woider, to swallow things down.
I'll uphold, in a week — by my troth I don't joke —
That our little Sal — shall fright all the town folk.
Come, get me some supper — But first let me peep
At the rest of my children — my calves, and my sheep.
WIFE. Ah! Jahn!
FARMER. Nay, cheer up — let not ghoasts trouble thee —
Look in thy glass — and *there* thou may'st see
I defie mortal man — to maake cuckold o' me.

Garrick had no intention of printing this interlude,

CREDULITY, SUPERSTITION, and FANATICISM.
A MEDLEY.

Believe not every Spirit but try the Spirits whether they are of God; because many false Prophets are gone out into the World. 1 John Ch. 4. v. 1.

Designed and Engraved by W.ᵐ Hogarth.     Publish'd as the Act directs March 5ᵗ. 1762.

7. 'Credulity, Superstition, and Fanaticism. A Medley',
by William Hogarth, 1762

though it was highly popular, but as Hogarth had made another sketch of him in the role, this time surrounded by his family, he printed it for the sake of using Hogarth's sketch as the frontispiece, and inscribed the piece to Hogarth 'as a faint testimony of the sincere esteem which the writer bears him, both as a man and an artist'.

Hogarth was one of the artists to depict Garrick in the role of the Farmer; another was Johann Zoffany, then a young and unknown immigrant from Bavaria. Zoffany's painting of Garrick in *The Farmer's Return from London* was so expressive and well executed that it immediately made his name upon being exhibited at the Society of Arts in April 1762. Horace Walpole even preferred Zoffany's to Hogarth's interpretation, and the *St. James's Chronicle*'s enthusiastic notice of it expressed the general admiration of the public: 'The painter absolutely transports us in imagination back again to the theatre. We see our favourite Garrick in the act of saying, *for* yes, *she knocked* once — *and for* no, *she knocked* twice. And we see the wife and children — as we saw them on the stage — in terror and amazement; such strong likenesses has the painter exhibited of the several performers that played the characters.'

Having once begun to ridicule the Ghost, Garrick brought her in to the 'Prologue upon Prologues', which he wrote to be spoken by the comedian, Thomas King, at King's benefit on March 30. After a few jokes, made with his usual ease, both of manner and metre, he continued:

> These facts laid down, then thus I reason:
> — Wit in a prologue's out of season —
> Yet still will you for jokes sit watching
> Like Cock-Lane folks for Fanny's scratching.
> And here my simile's so fit!
> For Prologues are but Ghosts of wit;

Which mean to show their art and skill,
And scratch you to their author's will.
    In short, for reasons great and small,
'Tis better to have none at all:
Prologues and Ghosts — a paltry trade!
So let them both at once be *laid*!
Say but the word — give your commands —
We'll tie OUR prologue-monger's hands:
Confine these culprits (*holding up his hands*),
    bind 'em tight,
Nor girls can scratch, nor fools can write.

The third of the London theatres, the Little Theatre in
the Haymarket, was often used by Samuel Foote for his
displays of mimicry. Foote was a mimic of genius; a wit
who delighted especially in taking off his famous contemporaries and commenting upon the follies of the day.
When Boswell spoke highly of his 'singular talent of
exhibiting people' to Johnson, Johnson growled back,
'Sir, it is not a talent, it is a vice; it is what others abstain
from. It is not comedy, which exhibits the character of a
species, as that of a miser gathered from many misers: it
is farce, which exhibits individuals.' Foote purposely
sought the acquaintance of those whom he intended to
represent in order to study them, and one of his intended
victims had been Johnson himself, but he wisely dropped
his plan. 'Did he not think of exhibiting you, Sir?' Boswell asked, with affected innocence. 'Sir, fear restrained
him; he knew I would have broken his bones', was the
answer.

    The Ghost was exactly the kind of topic that Foote
delighted to take off, and his pleasure would be increased
by so many of the clergy being involved. He could display
his infidelity without fear of legitimate censure, even if
he was, in Johnson's opinion, 'an infidel as a dog is an
infidel; that is to say he has never thought upon the

subject'. Foote's spleen was heightened by his having had to modify his satire on the Methodists when his farce of the *Minor* was produced in 1760.

Foote's performance was called 'Lectures on Oratory', thereby taking off the very popular series of lectures on oratory being given at this time by the veteran actor, Thomas Sheridan, and was held at the Haymarket Theatre on April 28.[1] The show opened with one of 'two well-dressed Smarts' sitting in a box suddenly beginning to wonder, as the curtain went up, and the candles were snuffed, whether he could really stand a lecture, having heard so many at Oxford. He wants his friend to leave and keep their appointment for dinner with two girls of the town, but when the girls are spyed in the gallery he agrees to stay, and after some more byplay Foote manages to begin his lecture, in which he runs through the various classes of orators.

Foote invites the audience to imagine they are attending at an imaginary court of justice, and, in order that the cause, too, may be ideal, he proposes to conduct 'the prosecution of an imaginary being; I mean the phantom of Cock-lane, a phenomenon that has much puzzled the brains, and terrified the minds of many of our fellow-subjects'. The clerk indicts Fanny for disturbing innocent simple people with her 'thumpings, knockings, scratch-ings and flutterings against doors, walls, wainscots, bed-steads, and bedposts'; Mr. Prosequi, her counsel, objects that she can only be tried by her equals, a jury of ghosts; the prosecuting Serjeant insists that she has foregone such a privilege by manifesting herself physically; Shadrach Bodkin, a Methodist tailor from Norwich, tries to refute him by witnessing that her noises were 'the very same thumps, scratches, and knocks, I have felt on my breast

[1] The text was published under the title of *The Orators*, 1762.

bone from the spirit within me'; and, lastly, Peter Paragraph, a newspaper editor, tells how he hired two hack
writers, at nine shillings a night, to sit up at Parsons's and
ask questions. In conclusion, Foote gave some 'particular
hints' on the manner of examining witness, taking as his
example a counsellor in 'the celebrated trial of Elizabeth
Canning', thus linking together again the two impostures,
which had been so frequently compared. The scene
changes and another theme is taken up. The piece was
very popular, but its success depended upon Foote himself, rather than on his text, even more a vehicle than
*The Farmer's Return* for a singular talent.

Elizabeth Canning is one of the few impostors not
directly introduced by Hogarth into his print 'Credulity,
Superstition, and Fanaticism; a Medley', published at
the end of April 1762. Hogarth had already been working
on an engraving, entitled 'Enthusiasm Delineated'. Its
intention was, in his own words, 'to give a lineal repre-
sentation of the strange effects of literal and low concep-
tions of sacred beings, as also of the idolatrous tendency
of pictures in churches and prints in religious books'.
The scene is inside a church and as the congregation
listen to the preacher thundering from the pulpit they
fondle or gorge themselves on gingerbread images of the
saints. Hogarth had recently drawn Garrick as the
Farmer, and with his head full of the Ghost and seeing in
it a perfect opportunity to vent his dislike of pious
knavery and devout irrationality, he quickly altered
'Enthusiasm Delineated' to express the theme started by
the Ghost.

The scene is the same, a church. A clergyman ex-
pounds the text 'I speak as a fool' with such violence that
his wig flies off to reveal the tonsure of the Jesuit and his
gown falls open to show the Harlequin's jacket under-

neath. Among the congregation is Mary Tofts, sprawling in a fit while the rabbits scamper out from under her skirts, and the Boy of Bilsdon spewing up his pins. The various emblems include a thermometer for measuring enthusiasm. The figure at the top of the column is the 'Drummer of Tedworth', and below it are representations of Fanny, with her hammer in her hand, and of Elizabeth Parsons in bed. The thermometer stands on copies of Wesley's *Sermons* and Glanvill's book *On Witches*, and the scale, attached at the bottom to a heart and losing itself at the top in clouds, measures both ways; upwards, from 'Luke Warm' through 'Love Heat', 'Lust', 'Extacy', and 'Convulsion Fits' to 'Madness'; and downwards, from 'Low Spirits', 'Sorrow', 'Agony', 'Settled Grief', 'Despair', and 'Madness' to 'Suicide'. A Turk looking in through a window from outside and grinning as he placidly smokes his pipe is comment enough on the disgraceful fantasy of the scene.

Another print, 'English Credulity, or the Invisible Ghost', by a far less accomplished artist than Hogarth, depicted the room in Cock Lane, with Elizabeth and her little sister put to bed. The various clergymen in the room comment appropriately, in the style of the comic strip. Blind Sir John Fielding, who is being led into the room, exclaims, 'I should be glad to see this Spirit', but his attendant warns him, 'Your Worship had better get your warrant backed by his Lordship', meaning that as a Middlesex magistrate, Sir John could not issue a warrant for arrest without it being endorsed by the Lord Mayor. Samuel Foote is also shown, exclaiming: 'Yea, if it had happen'd sooner 'twould have serv'd me for a new Character in the Lyar; the Story would tell better than the Cat and Kittens.' The 'cat and kittens' was one incident in a lying adventure told by Young Wilding,

the hero of Foote's comedy of *The Liar*, first performed
shortly before the coming of the Ghost. On the wall of
the room there hang two prints; one showing Bet Canning being succoured by an angel — for how else could
she had lived a month without food? — and the other
the 'Bottle Conjurer'. The Bottle Conjurer was one of
the most imaginative and successful hoaxes of the century. In January 1749 an advertisement appeared in the
newspapers to the effect that on the 16th January, at the
New Theatre in the Haymarket, a person would disappear into a wine bottle placed on a table in the middle
of the stage. He would sing from it and the audience
would be permitted to handle it while he was inside. He
also promised to play on a common walking-stick any
instrument then in use, and, in private seances, for a
gratuity, to raise the spirit of any departed loved one.
The theatre was packed, the Duke of Cumberland being
among the distinguished audience present, and when
nothing at all happened and no one appeared on the stage,
the hoaxed tore the interior of the theatre to pieces out of
chagrin. 'English Credulity' makes the only reference
associating the Conjurer and the Ghost.

'The Cock lane Ghost or the invisible humm bug for
the Year 1762' is the title of another print, similar in
style to 'English Credulity'. The child's room, with the
child abed, is again the scene, and a crowd of spectators
presses towards the bed, making appropriately cynical or
wondering comments. But the best of these popular
satirical prints was 'The Cock Lane Uproar', which is
divided into two scenes — Miss Parsons's bedroom and
the vaults of St. John's, Clerkenwell. The bedroom is
compared in the legend to the stage, and as Missy exclaims from the blankets that she feels 'the mouse', a mixed
audience of the credulous and the curious crowd about

her. A print of Mary Toft, the Rabbit Woman, is shown hanging on the wall. In the second scene, the committee of investigation, with Stephen Aldrich at the head, stands ready to descend into the glooms of the vault where Fanny Lynes was laid.

The Ghost was frequently ridiculed in verse, as well as in prose and on the stage and in prints. The *Public Advertiser* for February 5 carried some verses, supposedly written from Oxford, which described how 'Popish ignorance' had once been dispelled by the revival of learning and if it had returned and was no longer susceptible to the same cure, there yet remained a better trick:

> Should Latin, Greek, and Hebrew fail,
> I know a charm which *must* prevail:
> Take but an ounce of Common Sense,
> 'Twill scare the Ghosts, and drive 'em hence.

A tale, 'The Haunted Inn; or, A Counterpart to the late Cock Lane Ghost', written in the style of Dryden's fables, appeared in *Lloyd's Evening Post* for March 3 to 5, and told how a guest sleeping in the haunted room in an inn, once a ruined mansion, in the middle of the Forest of Arden, was led by a ghost to the discovery of buried treasure. The treasure turned out to be a 'golden mark' — its value can be left to the reader. The *London Chronicle's* contribution on March 16–18 to the anthology of verses inspired by the Ghost was more lively and topical than many others:

> I sing of that wonderful thing call'd a Ghost,
> Which late in Cocklane, we are told, rul'd the roast.
> A something, a nothing, yet mark'd with a name,
> Which some for believing their neighbours do blame,
> Whilst in private they'll own that their thoughts are the same...
> Now would I submit to the judgment of all
> Who ever drew breath since our first parent's fall,

If this *visible* name [apparition] can or ought to be given
To a thing, which has never been *seen* by man living;
But has only bamboozel'd by scratches and knocks
A set of old wives, silly peers, and mad bucks,
Who willing to try what their foolships could do
Repair'd to Cock-lane with a hallabalow;
Where Fanny, delighted to find the room fill'd
With shallow-brain'd asses, more afraid than good-will'd,
To discover the cheat, began her old pranks,
With a furious scratching against one of the planks,
That form'd the dire wainscot . . .

The best of the verses to appear in a newspaper was a ballad, 'The Ghost of Cock Lane', printed in the *St. James Chronicle* for the March, and is worth quoting in full:

There's a Place in this Town to which all do repair,
'Tis well known as the Sun, and as common as Air,
It has Plenty of Names, but to make it more plain,
(You may guess at the Reason) they call it *Cock-Lane*.
*Derry Down, &c.*

This Place, which before from the Time of the Flood
Was occupied ever by good Flesh and Blood,
Now laments all its jolly Inhabitants lost,
And is haunted and teaz'd by a terrible *Ghost*.
*Derry Down, &c.*

The World is alarm'd at so dreadful a Case,
Which threatens Destruction to all human Race;
For who will the Regions of *Cock-Lane* explore,
If a damnable Ghost is to stand at the Door?
*Derry Down, &c.*

The sorrowful Neighbours, of Ruin afraid,
Beadles, Watchmen, and Constables, call to their Aid,
But in Spite of the Watchmen, the Ghost goes at large, —
For taking of Ghosts is not in their Charge.
*Derry Down, &c.*

The Danger now calls for a Magistrate's Care,
And the terrify'd Women implore the Lord Mayor,
Pray, my Lord, bring your Mace, and your Sword, and your
   Chain,
For, believe us, a Ghost is crept into *Cock-Lane*.
                             *Derry Down, &c.*

His Lordship wou'd grant his Assistance he said,
But Sir Crisp and the Gypsey ran strong in his Head;
For unnatural Culprits he car'd not to search,
And it being a Ghost it belong'd to the Church.
                             *Derry Down, &c.*

The Clergy assembled a Hero to find,
Who in Fetters this Dragon of Wantley wou'd bind;
The Dragon once mentioned, up starts to their Call
Parson Moore, a Descendant of Moore of Morehall.
                             *Derry Down, &c.*

I come, quoth the Parson, whatever may hap,
For the Sake of my Country I'll stand in the Gap:
But prepare me a Bed, and a pretty young Maid,
For it is by this Means that the Ghost must be laid.
                             *Derry Down, &c.*

And lest there should be a Discovery made
How the Doctor conducted this Ghost-catching Trade,
The Lights were put out — but for Fear of a Hum,
The Ladies of Quality staid in the Room.
                             *Derry Down, &c.*

His Brethren, the Clergy, did likewise attend,
And with Prayers and with Vows did their Hero befriend;
Then bidding Defiance to Danger and Pain,
The Doctor jump'd merrily into *Cock-Lane*.
                             *Derry Down, &c.*

'Twould delight you to see how the Process went on,
There was Scratching, and Knocking, and Squeaking, and
   Fun;

When back comes the Doctor, and said with a Smile,
I've laid the proud Monster — at least for a while.
*Derry Down, &c.*

Yet tho' I have render'd it gentle and quiet,
Its Strength once recover'd, again it will riot;
But I'll batter it well from the Tail to the Snout;
So, by your Leave, Ladies, — I'll take t'other Bout.
*Derry Down, &c.*

And here we will stop — 'twould be Labour in vain,
If we wait till the Doctor has done with *Cock-Lane*;
But let us commend that Canonical Merit,
Which can conquer at once both the Flesh and the Spirit.
*Derry Down, &c.*

The ballad in the *St. James's Chronicle* is not a genuine
ballad of the kind written to be hawked about the streets;
it has the sophisticated fluent style of an accomplished
imitation, in the vein of Matt Prior; but luckily, one real
ballad, 'Cock-Lane, Humbug', complete with a crude
woodcut of Fanny in her shroud, with her hammer in
her hand, has survived for comparison. The ballad tells
simply but effectively the history of the affair and introduces two of the highlights, the visit of the Duke of York
and the descent into the vault of St. John's.

> The town it long has been in pain
> About the phantom in Cock-Lane,
> To find it out they strove in vain
>     Not one thing they neglected;
> They searched the bed and room compleat
> To see if there was any cheat,
> While little Miss that looks so sweet,
>     Was not the least suspected.
>
> Then soon the knocking it begun
> And then the scratching it wou'd come
> 'Twas pleased to answer any one,

And that was done by knocking;
If you was poison'd tell us true,
For yes knock one, for no knock two,
Then she knock'd I tell to you,
    What needs must make it shocking.

On Friday night as many know,
A noble Lord did thither go,
The Ghost its knocking wou'd not show
    Which made the Guest to mutter;
They being gone then one was there
Who always called it my dear,
Fanny was pleas'd 'tis very clear,
    And then began to flutter.

The Ghost some Gentlemen did tell,
If they would go to Clerkenwell,
Into the Vault where she did dwell,
    That they three knocks should hear sir.
On Monday night away they went,
The man accus'd he was present,
But all as death it was silent.
    The de'll a knock was there sir.

The Gentlemen return'd again,
And told young missy flat and plain,
She was the Agent of Cock-Lane,
    Who knock'd and scratch'd for Fanny.
'Twas false each person did agree,
Miss begg'd to go with her daddy
And then went into the Country
    To knock and scratch for Fanny.

All the verses in the newspapers were anonymous, but
some were published elsewhere and signed. George Alex-
ander Stevens, later famous for his 'Lecture upon Heads',
wrote a song — or, a 'peroration', as he preferred to call
it — specially to be sung by Kitty Clive at Drury Lane,
to the tune of 'Which nobody can deny'. Stevens was not

a song writer of great ability, though voluminous enough, but he illustrates the popular taste of the time. The following three of the eight stanzas of the song can be taken as representative — Clive would have lent grace of course to the most intolerable verses.

> With wonder each year we the old year out do,
> We scorn to consider how far a tale's true;
> 'Tis enough that 'tis talked of, and that the thing's new.
> Which nobody can deny . . .

> This Ghost is a Ghost of an odd composition,
> As he never appears, he is no apparition;
> But with blows like Free Masons makes known his condition.
> Which nobody, &c. . . .

> To hinder its blabbing there's one thing I wou'd do,
> And that, if they please to, all easily cou'd do,
> It is only behaving henceforth as we shou'd do.
> Which nobody, &c. . . .

Stevens was not even a versifier of pretensions, but the Reverend Thomas Denton, rector of Ashted, in Surrey, was a serious poet, though fame, alas! eluded him. *The House of Superstition, A Vision*, a Spenserian imitation, which he published in 1762, does not mention the Ghost, but was inspired by it. The argument is one with which those who had followed the Ghost in print were already familiar: Popish Superstition, in company with Ignorance, Error, Prejudice, Tyranny, Penance, Indulgence, and Persecution, is put to flight by Reform and Learning, personified by John Wycliffe. A pity that Denton's genius fell considerably short of his theme, even with the added buoyancy of Spenser.

Stevens and Denton and the newspaper versifiers were hardly able to uphold the honour of verse in a company that already included Johnson and Horace Walpole,

Garrick, Foote, and Hogarth, and, by proxy, John Wesley. But verse had no need to despair; a poet was already waiting in the wings, watching with amusement and ready to pounce.

# VIII

## A CAESARIAN OPERATION

CHARLES CHURCHILL had made his reputation within a year as being the finest and most dangerous satirist to have appeared since the death of Pope. His satire on the contemporary stage, *The Rosciad*, had been published in March 1761 and had already run through five editions. *The Apology*, a sharp and skilful rejoinder to the charge brought by the *Critical Review* that *The Rosciad* was the work of the triumvirate of wits, Robert Lloyd, George Colman and Bonnell Thornton, had been published in May and it, too, was in its fifth edition. Churchill had published at his own expense, having turned down an offer of five guineas for the copyright of *The Rosciad*, and the poems had brought him affluence as well as notoriety, metamorphosing an impoverished parish priest into a man about town. When he attended the theatre he still affected clerical black, but at the other resorts he dressed in the fashion. 'Let me see', said old John Taylor, trying to remember Churchill's appearance when, as a young man, he was introduced to the poet at Vauxhall; 'his coat was blue, edged with a narrow gold lace; a buff waistcoat; but I won't be certain whether that was laced or not — I rather think it was not. He had black silk small-clothes, white silk stockings, small silver shoe-buckles, and a gold-laced three-cornered hat.' The very antithesis, and not only in dress but through and through, of a droning Methodist.

*The Rosciad* was written in defence of Garrick. Imagining a competition for the chair once occupied by Roscius, the great Roman actor, Churchill considered each contender in turn and savagely and wittily demolished the pretensions of any who might be considered as seriously challenging Garrick's claim to pre-eminence. The town was delighted; by the scarifying attack itself, by the independence and freshness of the criticism, by the aptness with which the mannerisms and affectations of the actors were caught, and by the adeptness of the powerful heroic couplets. He struck so hard at some players that he drove Thomas Davies off the stage, in terror at his appearance in the front row of the pit, where he stood grasping the spikes which separated the audience from the stage, in his anxiety to see. He was at least safe from a cudgelling for he was a bruiser in frame as well as mentality.

The long delay that followed the publication of his third poem, *Night*, in November 1761, and its marked inferiority to his two earlier satires, were leading his critics to assert that he had already written himself out. But Churchill was far from asleep; he had found a subject which exactly suited his topical genius. He was hard at work on a satire on the Ghost.

Churchill must certainly have visited Fanny himself and may have watched Kent's descent into the vault on February 1. Realizing that success would depend on promptitude, he was ready to publish the first two Books of his new poem, *The Ghost*, by the first week of March. He may have been helped by having on hand part of a satire on superstition entitled *The Fortune Teller*, which he is supposed to have written years before when he began as a curate; but in fact the structure of *The Ghost* is so simple and the octo-syllabic verse so readily composed that the writing would naturally have proceeded with great rapidity.

The first Book is a conventional survey of the progress of superstition from the time of the Chaldees down to Churchill's own day, and introduces many of the stock figures who were brought in to discussions of the Ghost.

> England, a happy land we know,
> Where Follies naturally grow,

is sufficient to excuse the appearance of Mary Toft and Bet Canning, and to warrant an attack on the Methodists for credulity and hypocrisy. The second Book is equally digressive; contemporary reviewers were quick to point out the apparent similarity in method and manner between *The Ghost* and *Tristram Shandy*, well launched on its triumphal career; but it is primarily concerned to make fun of Aldrich's committee of investigation. The descent into the vault provides a natural climax. All the principals were satirized for credulity or duplicity, but the reader's attention inevitably falls first on the character of Johnson.

Any satire on the Ghost could hardly have omitted Johnson, but Churchill is believed to have had more personal reasons for attacking him. Boswell became one of Churchill's admirers and when he met him in 1763, in company with John Wilkes and Robert Lloyd, he felt, with his usual self-complacence, that he was got 'into the middle of the London Geniuses'. He once managed to sit beside the poet 'just at the spikes' at the theatre, and 'was vain to be seen talking with that great bard'. He was consequently anxious to learn from Johnson himself the cause of Churchill's quarrel with him, and when

The Farmer's Return.

W.ᵐ Hogarth.delin.                    James Basire.Sculp.

8. 'David Garrick as the Farmer', by William Hogarth

(From Garrick's *The Farmer's Return from London*, 1762)

Johnson attacked Churchill's poetry, Boswell suggested that he was hardly a fair judge as he himself had been a victim.

> Nay, Sir, I am a very fair judge [Johnson retorted]. He did not attack me violently till he found I did not like his poetry; and his attack on me shall not prevent me from continuing to say what I think of him, from an apprehension that it may be ascribed to resentment. No, Sir, I called the fellow a blockhead at first, and I will call him a blockhead still. However, I will acknowledge that I have a better opinion of him now, than I once had; for he has shewn more fertility than I expected. To be sure, he is a tree that cannot produce good fruit: he only bears crabs. But, Sir, a tree that produces a great many crabs is better than a tree which produces only a few.

Churchill thrice brought Johnson directly into the second Book. He appears once as 'our letter'd Polypheme' — referring to his blind eye — the cowardly patron of the plagiarist, William Lauder. He reappears farther on as '*Immane* Pomposo', the importer of 'crabbed foreign words', an old charge revived; and lastly, he is given a character and ridiculed:

> Pomposo (insolent and loud,
> Vain idol of a *scribbling* crowd,
> Whose very name inspires an awe,
> Whose ev'ry word is Sense and Law,
> For what his Greatness hath decreed,
> Like Laws of Persia and of Mede,
> Sacred thro' all the realm of *Wit*,
> Must never of Repeal admit;
> Who, cursing flatt'ry, is the tool
> Of ev'ry fawning flatt'ring fool;
> Who Wit with jealous eye surveys,
> And sickens at another's praise;
> Who, proudly seiz'd of *Learning's* throne,
> Now damns all Learning but his own;

Who scorns those common wares to trade in,
*Reas'ning, Convincing,* and *Persuading,*
But makes each Sentence current pass
With *Puppy, Coxcomb, Scoundrel, Ass;*
For 'tis with *him* a certain rule,
The Folly's prov'd, when he calls Fool;
Who, to increase his native strength,
Draws words, six syllables in length,
With which, assisted with a frown
By way of Club, he knocks us down;
Who 'bove the Vulgar dares to rise,
And sense of *Decency* defies,
For this same *Decency* is made
Only for Bunglers in the trade;
And, like the *Cobweb Laws,* is still
Broke thro' by *Great Ones* when they will) —
POMPOSO, with *strong sense* supplied,
Supported, and confirmed by *Pride,*
His Comrades' terrors to beguile,
*Grinn'd horribly a ghastly smile:*
Features so horrid, were it light,
Would put the Devil himself to flight.

Johnson could afford to shrug off such an attack — 'I wished the man a dinner and sat still' — and his friends would know that none of the lines was really penetrative, but many of Johnson's superficial mannerisms and his appearance were well caught, and the whole impression is, though brutal, effective and amusing.

The book ends with the anticlimax of Pomposo's and his two companions' united descent into the vault:

> Silent all three went in, about
> All three turn'd silent, and came out.

By the time Churchill had published the first two Books, the Ghost had ceased to knock, but he had not finished with the poem. The accession of George III in 1760 had seen the beginning of a fundamental change in English politics. A coalition of great Whig families had governed the country ever since the accession of George I in 1714, at first under the long leadership of Sir Robert Walpole and later under the direction of William Pitt and the Duke of Newcastle; but George III, brought up on the ideas of the Tory theorist, Lord Bolingbroke, and tutored by the Earl of Bute, had determined to govern by means of the Tories, the 'King's friends'. Portents of the coming struggle for power had appeared at the very beginning of the reign, when slogans were chalked up on the walls protesting against the 'petticoat government' of the Dowager Princess of Wales, the King's mother, and the dominance of the 'Scotch favourite', Lord Bute, popularly supposed to be intimate with the Princess; but the brunt of the popular dislike of the new arrangement was not felt until Pitt's resignation on October 5, 1761, and Lord Bute's appointment as First Lord of the Treasury on May 29, 1762.

The day of Bute's appointment, Tobias Smollett published the first number of *The Briton*, a paper written specifically in support of the Bute Administration. Within the week he was answered by *The North Briton*, conducted by John Wilkes, with the help of Churchill. When Churchill met Wilkes is uncertain, but in his new life about town he would have been bound to have come into touch with one of the most licentious and charming and ugliest men of his age. Wilkes boasted that he could seduce any woman in spite of his appearance, and even men as violently opposed to his political principles and his morals as Johnson succumbed to his charm. The dinner at which Wilkes successfully paid court to Johnson is one of the most famous scenes in Boswell's biography, an interview which Boswell arranged with the idea of its description in mind.

Wilkes gave Churchill exactly what he required as a satirist, an introduction into politics at a time when political feeling ran as high as at any other time in English history, short of civil war; and from the occasion of their meeting Churchill became his devoted henchman and propagandist, lending his verse in support of his cause. As a poet, he soon found that the Ghost itself was an inadequate subject once popular interest in it began to wane; but *The Ghost* as a Shandean vehicle for random satire had certain merits.

He found difficulty in writing the third Book, in view of the distractions of both his private life and politics. 'Pray remember the ghost for me to-night', Wilkes wrote to him on June 15, 1762, when asking him to correct a number of *The North Briton* and reminding him that they were to meet at Medmenham Abbey, the seat of Sir Francis Dashwood and the scene of the notorious revels of the Hell Fire Club.

> Where is the Ghost. [Churchill replied, on July 15] Faith I cannot tell — the flesh has engross'd so much of my care that I have never once thought of the Spirit . . . In your's you tell me you engaged with — I could not understand it, my Lindamira says it must be with Old Scratch, with whom, judging you by me, she supposes us both to be on good terms. I rather think you meant it a hint for me to fill up a blank, and she seems to like the interpretation, and looks towards the bed.

The third Book proceeded apace.

Johnson himself was greatly affected by the accession of the new King. He had been all his life a devoted and outspoken Tory, but it was not for his politics that he was rewarded. In the summer of 1762, after Lord Bute's elevation to power, he was approached to ascertain if he would be prepared to accept a pension. He was firmly assured that it was being given for his past services to literature, not with the intention of coaxing his pen into the service of the new administration. He was in a special difficulty, for he had notoriously defined *pension* in his *Dictionary* as being generally understood in England 'to mean pay given to a state hireling for treason to his country', and pensioner as 'one who is supported by an allowance paid at the will of another; a dependant'. But after consulting with his friends as to the propriety of accepting, he took their advice and accepted what had been freely offered, without conditions.

An annual income of three hundred pounds was a large sum to Johnson, inured as he was to poverty; and by removing him from necessity, the only motive for writing, in his opinion, it deferred the chance of his completing his edition of Shakespeare, as often postponed as it had been promised. He had issued proposals for an edition as long ago as 1756 and had taken in subscriptions, but publication was repeatedly delayed. One of his friends remarked that 'he never thinks of working if he has a couple of guineas in his pocket'; and with three hundred pounds a year coming in, his pocket was unlikely to be ever empty.

In the third Book of *The Ghost*, completed at last, and published in October 1762, Churchill cursorily touched on his ostensible subject, mocking particularly at the intervention of Sir Samuel Fludyer, the Lord Mayor, by this time a declared supporter of the Bute administration. For the rest he struck at random, wherever he found a subject to mind. But Johnson himself as Pomposo was still an essential character, and Churchill seized upon his receipt of a pension as the most convenient weapon of attack. The pension he interpreted as a public mark of loss of integrity; and worse! of a renegade, for had not

Johnson been a consistent supporter of the House of
Stuart, and had he not in effect been bribed to transfer
his allegiance to the House of Hanover? In confirmation
of Johnson's lack of principle he cited against him his
taking of subscriptions to his edition of Shakespeare,
without any intention of delivering the book.

> Horrid, *unwieldy, without Form,*
> *Savage,* as OCEAN in a Storm,
> *Of size prodigious,* in the rear,
> *That Post of Honour,* should appear
> POMPOSO; *Fame* around should tell
> How he a slave to int'rest fell,
> How for *Integrity* renown'd,
> Which Booksellers have often found,
> He for *Subscribers* baits his hook,
> And takes their cash — but where's the Book?
> No matter where — *Wise* Fear, we know,
> Forbids the robbing of a Foe,
> But what, to serve our private ends,
> Forbids the cheating of our Friends?
> No Man alive, who would not swear
> All's *safe,* and therefore *honest* there.
> For spite of all the learned say,
> If we to Truth attention pay,
> The word *Dishonesty* is meant
> For nothing else but *Punishment.* . .
> How to all Principles untrue,
> Nor fix'd to *old* Friends, nor to *New,*
> He damns the *Pension* which he takes,
> And loves the STUART he forsakes.

Johnson may have really remarked, as he is said to have
done, after reading this invective, 'If I can't bear this I
don't deserve my money'. The observation is at least in
character. He might affect unconcern, but for his friends
who loved him, the attack was unbearable, especially
since it called his probity into question. As Saunders

Welch had warned him, his association with the Ghost was bringing him into ridicule; and not alone on the score of credulity and superstition: in the political tension that followed Bute's appointment, the only object was to damage those on the other side by any means possible. Johnson might disregard Churchill, but he could not overlook his friends, and, as Boswell observed on the edition of Shakespeare, 'we may almost conclude that the Caesarian operation was performed by the knife of Churchill, whose upbraiding satire, I dare say, made Johnson's friends urge him to dispatch'. Boswell implies, however, that delivery was quicker than happened in fact; subscribers had still to wait until October 1765 before receiving their copies. Churchill had by then been dead and buried for a year.

# IX

## THE JUDGES ARE MET

BEFORE the publication of the third Book of *The Ghost* the Cock Lane conspirators had been brought up for trial. The case came on at the Guildhall before Lord Mansfield on July 10. The Reverend John Moore, Richard James, the tradesman, Richard Parsons, Mrs. Parsons, and Mary Frazer were in the dock. The trial began at ten o'clock in the morning, on an information 'brought by William Kent against the above defendants for a conspiracy to take away his life by charging him with the murder of Frances Lynes by giving her poison whereof she died'. The court was crowded with spectators. Kent gave evidence first. He related the history of his marriage and his later intimacy with Fanny, and went on to tell of her death and her bizarre resurrection as 'Scratching Fanny'. James Franzen blurted out his fearful experience of the Ghost, and Esther Carlisle — 'Carrots' — corroborated his story as far as it related to herself, and impressed the court with her simple sturdy decency. Dr. Cooper repeated what he had already stated in his affidavit and affirmed that from the first he had believed the knockings and scratchings in Cock Lane to be a trick. James Jones confirmed Cooper's account of Fanny's illness. Elizabeth Dancey gave evidence to the effect that the Ghost had claimed to be the spirit of Fanny Lynes, and Missiter described his experiment of slinging the girl in a hammock and how he had caught her in the act of secreting the piece of wood with which she had later knocked. William Bristow, the publisher of *The Mystery Revealed*, acknowledged that he had inserted the list of questions put to the Ghost, with her answers, in the *Public Ledger*. The prosecution's last witness, Charles Say, the publisher of the *Ledger*, stated that Richard James was responsible for the advertisements complained about, appearing on January 23 and February 14 in the paper.

The defence called a number of people, neighbours and sympathizers, who had entertained the girl and still believed that the knockings were preternatural, or could otherwise support the view that there had been no imposture. Bateman Griffiths, the carpenter who had taken down Parsons's wainscot, Mr. Gammon, the apothecary, Elizabeth Parsons's attendant during her fits in 1760, and Catherine Friend, the lodger who had left Parsons's in alarm at the Ghost, were all called. They were followed in turn by Miss Bray. 'I do not think the noise was made by the girl', Miss Bray obstinately affirmed, 'but by a Ghost or some other preternatural means.' And Hannah Darking was even more emphatic; when the court burst out laughing at her credulity, she exclaimed angrily, 'I assure you, gentlemen, it is no laughing matter, whatever you may think of it.' Jane Armstrong, Mr. Bray and his servant, and Mr. Bruin were equally of the Ghost's party. Mr. Bruin had been convinced by it because it had told him something it could have learnt only by preternatural means. He had given some money to a poor acquaintance and upon asking the Ghost, how many coins? it had knocked once — correct! The prosecuting counsel interjected that 'he should have asked what number of miles it was from London to Newcastle; it

would have been the likeliest way to find them out.' The
Reverend Mr. Broughton and the Reverend Mr. Ross —
the 'philosophical' enquirer — were on hand, too, to
affirm that Fanny still enjoyed their pious patronage.
When Ross told the court of the questions he had put to
the Ghost, Lord Mansfield asked, 'Whether he thought
he had puzzled the Ghost, or the Ghost had puzzled him?'
Dr. Nichols, Dr. Birch, Dr. Burton, and Daniel Pon-
ton, in the Commission of Peace for Surrey, and many
others, appeared for John Moore and gave him 'as good
a character as any man could have'. But Moore had
even stronger support at hand, though he was stopped
from availing himself of it. According to Horace Walpole, Moore had the impudence to present a letter to
Lord Mansfield on the bench from Thomas Secker,
Archbishop of Canterbury, 'interceding on his behalf,
for Secker had a fellow feeling for hypocritical enthusiasm.
The Chief Justice put the letter into his pocket unopened,
saying it was impossible it could relate to the cause in
question.' Several appeared on behalf of James; and those
who spoke up for Parsons, while acknowledging that he
was very drunken, could not believe him guilty of such a
conspiracy.

Churchill himself was among the fashionable audience
and wrote in high spirits to John Wilkes: 'Last Saturday
I heard the Trial of the Conspirators relative to Miss
Fanny and was much entertained. They proposed to
bring the Girl into Court, but my Lord looking in that way
which is called looking we don't know how, and applying
his hand to that part of the body where fools they say are
better provided than men of sense, significantly declared
that he would advise them not to bring her in, for, quoth
my Lord, I find I shall certainly beat her.' Churchill
ended his note by expressing how much he was looking

forward to meeting Wilkes, for though his devotion to the reigning doxy had made him more temperate, he was 'above being thoroughly sober with an honest fellow' like Wilkes.

The trial lasted the whole day, from ten o'clock in the morning until half past nine at night. At one point in the proceedings Fanny herself sounded to have arrived. A violent noise in an adjoining room terrified the credulous out of their wits, but it was found that a gentleman finding himself trapped on the roof had broken in a window trying to get down. Lord Mansfield took an hour and a half to sum up; the jury fifteen minutes to reach their verdict. Mr. Hall of Bucklersbury, foreman, rose and gave 'all guilty'.

On the following Monday, two other people, Richard Browne and the otherwise unidentified 'J. A. L.', responsible for publishing in the newspaper against Kent were tried before Lord Mansfield and found guilty.[1] They were later fined fifty pounds apiece.

The conspirators were not brought up to the Court of King's Bench for sentence until November 22, but a decision was then postponed to a later date, in the hope that they would agree to compound with Kent in the matter of damages. They were brought before the court again on January 27, and having been found to have failed to make satisfaction they were all committed to the King's Bench prison, to await sentence at the end of term. John Moore and Richard James appeared on February 11 and, having given Kent satisfaction to the amount of £588, they were reprimanded by Mr. Justice Wilmot and dismissed. The others appeared on the following day. Parsons was sentenced to two years' imprison-

---

[1] Browne was certainly one of the pair. I conjecture 'J. A. L.' to have been the other.

ment and to stand three times in the pillory; his wife to one year in prison; and Mary Frazer, the interpreter, to six months in Bridewell. Mr. Justice Wilmot, 'in a speech most excellently adapted to the occasion, expatiated on the indignity of such an imposture'. But Parsons was not to be silenced. He went out protesting that he had never had grounds for malice against Kent, not having been arrested by him for debt as had been reported. And as for the knockings, many people besides himself had heard them; if they had been given with a mallet they could not have been more distinct.

Parsons persuaded not only himself but many others that what he had heard was true, and when he stood in the pillory on March 16 for the first time, at the end of Cock Lane, he was very kindly treated and a 'handsome sum' was collected for him. How violent the mob could be with those guilty of crimes it detested is shown in the case of the man guilty of sodomy, who was killed as he stood in the pillory in April of the same year. Parsons stood again on March 30 at the Royal Exchange, and for the last time on April 8 at Charing Cross: on both occasions he was well treated and collections were taken up for him.

After the newspaper reports of Parsons in the pillory, all the conspirators disappeared; only John Moore's death in 1767 is reported. Richard James, Parsons and his wife, Mary Frazer and Browne, vanish into obscurity. Elizabeth Parsons raises the echo of a rap; she is supposed to have died at Chiswick in 1805, having been married twice. And accompanying them into oblivion went William Kent. The Ghost had often been compared to a theatrical entertainment, and as the curtain falls the actors disperse; the Cock Lane players disappear and only the memory of their performance remains.

# X

## A MOST IMPORTANT
## QUESTION

THE great figures who had become involved in the Ghost did not disappear. David Garrick had more than ten years left before his retirement to enjoy being the greatest actor of the British stage. Hogarth mistakenly involved himself directly in politics, and, choosing the opposite side, he clashed with Churchill and was savaged by him in *An Epistle to William Hogarth*, in ways that he found it hardest to bear. He made himself thoroughly miserable and died, by a curious coincidence, at almost the same time as his foe, once his ally in the fight against superstition.

Horace Walpole continued to laugh at folly and credulity and in 1794 had a fine story to tell of how the female figure which visited the Bishop of Chichester in the middle of the night turned out to be not a spirit, as he thought, but a wandering lunatic. 'I have known stories of ghosts, solemnly authenticated, less credible', Walpole added. But though he might mock as such apparitions, only two years after the affair in Cock Lane he published *The Castle of Otranto*, the first 'Gothic' romance. Among the preternatural marvels he recounted in that tale, a ghost like Fanny would have passed as an unexceptionable

his letters, point to the contradictions in his character —
and in the spirit of the age.

Charles Churchill could not forget the Ghost; he was
committed to adding a fourth book to his poem. When it
appeared in November 1763 it was found to be a long,
rambling excursion whose origins in a particular event
had been entirely lost. But he had been drawn by this
time into the centre of the violent political action fought
by Wilkes. He came close to arrest when Wilkes was
taken up on April 30, 1764, and confined in the Tower
for publishing the famous *North Briton*, No. 45. In this
intense excitement Churchill found full scope for his
truculent genius, and wrote the poems by which, after
*The Rosciad* and *The Apology*, he is best remembered: *The
Prophecy of Famine*, *An Epistle to William Hogarth*, and *The
Candidate*. But his extraordinary activity in these years,
joined to the wildness of his private life, burnt him out
and he died of a fever at Boulogne on November 4, 1764,
while on a visit to Wilkes, who had retreated to France.
He was thirty-three. His body was brought back to
Dover and buried under a stone inscribed with one of his
own lines, 'Life to the last enjoy'd, *here* Churchill lies'.
When he came to stand by that grave fifty years later,
Byron, on his way out of England for the last time, was
moved to write the melancholy touching poem that
begins:

> I stood beside the grave of him who blazed
> The comet of a season.

'I on my journey all alone proceed', Churchill wrote
prophetically in the poem he was still engaged on at the
time of his death. The same journey lay before Johnson,
and the thought of what might lie at the end troubled
him more deeply as the years passed. He continued to
search anxiously for proofs of the survival of the spirit

character. The novel, and his comments on the occult in after death. He still refused to be gulled, however, and the standards he had rigorously applied to the Cock Lane Ghost were those he insisted should be met.

He never gave up hope and it was John Wesley himself, as credulous as ever — though he needed no ghost to support his fervent belief in the immortality of the redeemed soul — who gave him an account of yet another spirit which seemed to satisfy his demands. 'Pray, Sir'; Boswell asked him in company on April 17, 1778; 'what has Wesley made of his story of a ghost?' 'Why, Sir, he believes it'; Johnson replied, 'but not on sufficient authority. He did not take time enough to examine the girl. . . . I am sorry that John did not take more pains to inquire into the evidence for it.' 'What, Sir! about a ghost?' Miss Seward exclaimed, astonished. 'Yes, Madam,' Johnson answered, with solemn vehemence; 'this is a question which, after five thousand years, is yet undecided; a question, whether in theology or philosophy, one of the most important that can come before the human understanding.'

Such were the tones that dignified and lent pathos and significance to the Ghost of Cock Lane.